Christian Politician

A Collection of Testimonies in Favor of religious Liberty

Christian Politician

A Collection of Testimonies in Favor of religious Liberty

ISBN/EAN: 9783337148249

Printed in Europe, USA, Canada, Australia, Japan

Cover: Foto ©ninafisch / pixelio.de

More available books at **www.hansebooks.com**

COLLECTION

OF

TESTIMONIES

IN FAVOR OF

RELIGIOUS LIBERTY,

IN THE CASE OF THE

DISSENTERS, CATHOLICS, and JEWS.

BY

A CHRISTIAN POLITICIAN.

Rixatur de lanâ fœpe caprinâ.
               Hor.

LONDON:

PRINTED IN THE YEAR 1790.
Sold by C. DILLY, Poultry; J. JOHNSON, St. Paul's Church-Yard;
and J. DEBRETT, Piccadilly.

PREFACE

IN this age it is still necessary to prove, that the wrath of man worketh not the righteousness of God. Streams of blood, desert countries, unanswered arguments, slowly teach men who are in possession of power, that Providence takes better methods for the Propagation of the true religion, than can be expected from the interference of its creatures.—— But we shall cease to be surprised at this obstinacy, if we recollect that the partisans of power, when they say that they are taking care of the concerns of God, think they are at the same moment taking care of their own.

In pleading for the Catholics I shall offend many Dissenters; and in pleading for the Jews, I shall offend many Dissenters and Catholics.—— But shall I in this offend the Deity, to whom Dissenters, Catholics, and Jews equally belong? I trust not. Men who are left without any other guide than their opinions, had need be tender, lest in the person of another they should persecute truth itself.——Besides is not charity an appendage of truth?

It is however chiefly in a political view that I have collected a few testimonies in favour of general religious liberty. Articles 2, 3, 9, and 21 are my own: Article 20 is an original by a friend: The rest speak for themselves.——As I conceived and executed the design of this collection within a few days, I shall be forgiven for its defects. I have omitted in compliment to prejudice, every thing written by the Dissenting Clergy or by profane persons,——But I trust there is enough produced to confound the religious Bigot; and to convince the Politician that to check religious discussion is favourable to the welfare of men neither here under his own government, nor hereafter under that of God.

February 1790.

TABLE OF CONTENTS.

Art.		Page
I.	THE Freeholder N° 21 and 47, written by Mr. Addison	1
II.	Remarks on the Debate in the House of Commons in 1787, on the Subject of the Sacramental Test Laws; with Hints concerning the Catholics, Jews, Marriage Service, &c. in a Letter to a Friend; including some Passages from M. Turgot	7
III.	Preface to the English Translation of Baron Born's Natural History of Monks, after the Linnæan System	28
IV.	Scheme by the Bishop of Clonfert for reforming the Irish Catholics	39
V.	Letter of Lord Mountgarret on the State of Church Affairs in Ireland	40
VI.	Arguments extracted from Bishop Hoadly's reply to Bishop Sherlock on the Sacramental Test Laws	46
VII.	Testimonies on the same Subject from Bishop Sherlock's Life, Dr. Sykes, Archdeacon Payley, and the late Earl of Chatham	52
VIII.	Arguments from Mr Locke's Letters on Toleration	56
IX.	Testimonies on the same Subject by Sir Josiah Child, Mr. Richard Jackson, M. P. deceased, Dr. Davenant, Archbishop Sharp, and the Author of Essays on Population	59
X.	The same, from Sir William Temple's Observations on the Netherlands	62
XI.	Arguments from a Work intitled, " Rights of the " Dissenters to a compleat Toleration asserted;" including Hints by Dr. Franklin and others	64
XII.	Earl Mansfield's Opinion on the Religious Liberty of the Dissenters, with Extracts from President de Thou referred to by him	75

CONTENTS.

Art.		Page
XIII.	Two Persian Letters by President Montesquieu, respecting religious Liberty and the Jews — —	79
XIV.	Mr. Necker's Opinion on religious Liberty — —	82
XV.	M. Rabaud de St. Etienne's Speech on the same Subject	83
XVI.	Measures of the National Assembly of France respecting Non-Catholics — — — — — —	85
XVII.	Act of the Assembly of Virginia in 1786, for establishing religious Freedom — — — — —	87
XVIII.	Parable against Persecution, imitated from a Jewish Tradition, by Dr. Franklin, with an Extract from the same Author — — — — — — —	88
XIX.	Addresses from the Quakers and Episcopalians of the Middle American States to General Washington, with his Answers — — — — — —	90
XX.	Facts and Observations respecting the Situation of the Jews in England — — — — — —	92
XXI.	Two Letters by a Christian Politician, which first appeared in the Public Advertiser, in February 1790	103

APPENDIX.

I.	The Case of the Protestant Dissenters, in 1790 — —	i
II.	History of the Test and Corporation Acts, extracted from "the Rights of the Dissenters, &c." — —	vi
III.	Protests in the House of Lords in Favor of the Dissenters	xiii
IV.	Also Resolutions in the House of Commons — — —	xi
V.	Also Petition by the Livery of London to the same Effect	xv
VI.	Testimonies of our Kings in Favor of the Dissenters for more than a Century — — — — — — —	xvi
VII.	Resolutions of the Committee of London Dissenters in 1790 — — — — — — — — —	xvii

ERRATA.

Page
6 Line 10 from the bottom, read "some part of the town or another."
75 Second line, Art. xii. after "after office" read "of sheriff."
79 At the end of the note, add "from the fathers of the church."
86 Put inverted commas to the numbered paragraphs, and dele the numbers.
xviii Appendix, in the title read "1790" for "1780."

ARTICLE I.

THE FREEHOLDER.†

Written by Mr. Addison N° 21, March 5, 1716.

FOR the honour of his Majesty and the safety of his government we cannot but observe, that those who have appeared the greatest enemies to both, are of that rank of men, who are commonly distinguished by the title of *Fox-hunters*. As several of these have had no part of their education in cities, camps, or courts, it is doubtful whether they are of greater ornament or use to the nation in which they live: It would be an everlasting reproach to politics, should such men be able to overturn an establishment, which has been formed by the wisest laws, and is supported by the ablest heads. The wrong notions and prejudices which cleave to many of these country gentlemen, who have always lived out of the way of being better informed, are not easy to be conceived by a person who has never conversed with them.

That I may give my readers an image of these rural statesmen, I shall, without farther preface, set down an account of a discourse I chanced to have with one of them some time ago.—I was travelling towards one of the remote parts of England, when about three o'clock in the afternoon, seeing a country gentleman trotting before me with a spaniel by his horse's side, I made up to him. Our conversation opened, as usual, upon the weather; in which we were unanimous; having both agreed that it was too dry for the season of the year.— My fellow-traveller, upon this, observed to me, that there had been no good weather since the Revolution. I was a little startled at so extraordinary a remark, but would not interrupt him, till he proceeded to tell me of the fine weather they used to have in king Charles the Second's reign. I only answered, that I did not see how the badness of the weather could be the king's fault:—and without waiting for his reply, asked him whose house it was we saw upon a rising ground at a little distance from us. He told me it belonged to an old fanatical

---

† 'The Freeholder (says Dr. Johnson) was undertaken in defence of the esta-
' blished government.---Bigotry itself must be delighted with the Tory Fox-
' hunter.'---N. B. Mr. Addison, who afterwards became Secretary of State, plainly shews that he considers the Dissenters to have been highly friendly to the Revolution, and the high-church party to have been its great opposers.

cur, Mr. Such-a-one; you muſt have heard of him, ſays he; he's one of the Rump. I knew the gentleman's character upon hearing his name, but aſſured him that to my knowledge he was a good churchman. Ah! ſays he with a kind of ſurprize; we were told in the country that he ſpoke twice, in the queen's time, againſt taking off the duties upon French claret.—This naturally led us into the proceedings of the late parliaments, upon which occaſion he affirmed roundly, that there had not been one good law paſſed ſince king William's acceſſion to the throne, except the act for preſerving the game.—I had a mind to ſee him out, and therefore did not care for contradicting him. Is it not hard, ſays he, that honeſt gentlemen, ſhould be taken into cuſtody of meſſengers to prevent them from acting according to their conſciences? But, ſays he, what can we expect when a parcel of factious ſons of whores—He was going on in a great paſſion, but chanced to miſs his dog, who was amuſing himſelf about a buſh, that grew at ſome diſtance behind us. He ſtood ſtill till he had whiſtled him up; when he fell into a long panegyrick upon his ſpaniel, who ſeemed indeed excellent in his kind: but I found the moſt remarkable adventure of his life was, that he had once like to have worried a diſſenting teacher. The maſter could hardly ſit on his horſe for laughing, all the while he was giving me the particulars of this ſtory; which I found had mightily endeared his dog to him, and as he himſelf told me, had made him a great favourite among all the honeſt gentlemen of the country.—We were at length diverted from this piece of mirth by a poſt-boy, who winding his horn at us, my companion gave him too or three curſes and left the way clear for him. I fancy, ſaid I, that poſt brings news from Scotland: I ſhall long to ſee the next printed Gazette. Sir, ſays he, I make it a rule never to believe any of your printed news. We never ſee, Sir, how things go, except now and then in Dyer's letter, and I read that more for the ſtyle than the news. The man has a clever pen it muſt be owned: But is it not ſtrange that we ſhould be making war upon Church of England men, with Dutch and Swiſs ſoldiers, men of anti-monarchical principles? theſe foreigners will never be loved in England, Sir; they have not that wit and good breeding that we have.— I muſt confeſs I did not expect to hear my new acquaintance value himſelf upon theſe qualifications, but finding him ſuch a critic upon foreigners, I aſked him if he had ever travelled; he told me, he did not know what travelling was good for, but to teach a man to ride the great horſe, to jabber French, and to talk againſt paſſive obedience: to which he added, that he ſcarce ever knew a traveller in his life who had not forſook his principles, and loſt his hunting-ſeat. For my part, ſays he, I and my father before me have always been for paſſive obedience, and ſhall be always for oppoſing a prince who makes uſe of miniſters that are of another opinion.—But where do you

intend

intend to inn to night? (for we were come in fight of the next town:) I can help you to a very good landlord, if you will go along with me. He is a lufty jolly fellow, that lives well, at leaft three yards in the girt, and the beft church of England man upon the road. I had a curiofity to fee this high-church inn-keeper, as well as to enjoy more of the converfation of my fellow-traveller; and therefore readily confented to fet our horfes together for that night.—As we rode fide by fide through the town, I was let into the characters of all the principal inhabitants whom we met in our way. One was a dog, another a whelp, another a cur, and another the fon of a bitch; under which feveral denominations were comprehended all that voted on the Whig fide in the laft election of burgeffes. As for thofe of his own party, he diftinguifhed them by a nod of his head, and afking them how they did by their chriftian names.—Upon our arrival at the inn, my companion fetched out the jolly landlord, who knew him by his whiftle. Many endearments and private whifpers paffed between them; though it was eafy to fee, by the landlord's fcratching his head, that things did not go to their wifhes.—The landlord had fwelled his body to a prodigious fize, and worked up his complexion to a ftanding crimfon, by his zeal for the profperity of the church; which he expreffed every hour of the day, as his cuftomers dropt in, by repeated bumpers. He had not time to go to church himfelf, but, as my friend told me in my ear, had headed the mob at the pulling down of two or three meeting-houfes. While fupper was preparing, he enlarged upon the happinefs of the neighbouring fhire; for, fays he, there is fcarce a Prefbyterian in the whole county, except the bifhop.—In fhort, I found by his difcourfe that he had learned a great deal of *politics*, but not one word of *religion*, from the parfon of his parifh; and indeed, that he had fcarce any other notion of religion, but that it confifted *in hating Prefbyterians*. I had a remarkable inftance of his notions in this particular. Upon feeing a poor decrepid old woman pafs under the window where we fat, he defired me to take notice of her; and afterwards informed me, that fhe was generally reputed a witch by the country people; but that for his part, he was apt to believe that fhe was a Prefbyterian.

Supper was no fooner ferved in, than he took occafion, from a fhoulder of mutton that lay before us, to cry up the plenty of England; which would be the happieft country in the world, provided we would live within ourfelves. Upon this he expatiated on the inconveniences of trade, that carried from us the commodities of our country, and made a parcel of upftarts as rich as men of the moft ancient families of England. He then declared frankly, that he had always been againft all treaties and alliances with foreigners; our wooden walls, fays he, are our fecurity, and we may bid defiance to the whole world; efpecially if they would attack us when the militia is out.—I ventured to reply, that I had as great an opinion of the English fleet as he had; but I could not see how they could be paid, and manned, and fitted out, unless we encouraged trade and navigation. He replied, with some vehemence, that he would undertake to prove, trade would be the ruin of the English nation. I would fain have put him upon it; but he contented himself with affirming it more eagerly; to which he added two or three curses upon the London merchants, not forgetting the directors of the Bank.—After supper he asked me if I was an admirer of punch; and immediately called for a sneaker. I took this occasion to insinuate the advantages of trade, by observing to him, that water was the only native of England that could be made use of on this occasion: but that the lemons, the brandy, the sugar, and the nutmeg, were all foreigners. This put him into some confusion; but the landlord, who overheard me, brought him off, by affirming that for constant use, there was no liquor like a cup of English water, provided it had malt enough in it. My squire laughed heartily at the conceit, and made the landlord sit down with us.—We sate pretty late over our punch; and amidst a great deal of improving discourse, drank the health of several persons in the country whom I had never heard of, that, they both assured me, were the ablest statesmen in the nation: and of some Londoners, whom they extolled to the skies for their wit, and who I knew passed in town for silly fellows.—It being now midnight, and my friend perceiving by his almanack that the moon was up, he called for his horses, and took a sudden resolution to go to his house, which was at three miles distance from the town, after having bethought himself that he never slept well out of his own bed. He shook me very heartily by the hand at parting, and discovered a great air of satisfaction in his looks, that he had met with an opportunity of showing his parts, and left me a much wiser man than he found me.

The Freeholder Nº 47, June 1, 1716.

I Question not but most of my readers will be very well pleased to hear, that my friend the *Fox-hunter*, of whose arrival in town I gave notice in my forty-fourth paper, is become a convert to the present establishment, and a good subject of king George. The motives to his conversion shall be the subject of this paper; as they may be of use to other persons who labour under those prejudices and prepossessions, which hung so long upon the mind of my worthy friend. These I had an opportunity of learning the other day, when, at his request, we took a ramble together to see the curiosities of this great town.

The first circumstance, as he ingenuously confessed to me (while we were in the coach together) which helped to disabuse him, was seeing king Charles the First on horseback at Charing-cross; for he was sure that prince could never have kept his seat there, had the stories been true he had heard in the country, that forty-one was come about again.

He owned to me, that he looked with horror on the new church that is half built in the Strand, as taking it at first to be half demolished: But upon enquiry of the workmen, was agreeably surprized to find that instead of pulling it down, they were building it up; and that fifty more were raising in other parts of the town.

To these I must add a third circumstance which I find had no small share in my friend's conversion. Since his coming to town, he chanced to look into the church of St. Paul about the middle of Sermon-time; where, having first examined the dome to see if it stood safe, (for the screw-plot still run in his head,) he observed, that the Lord-Mayor, Aldermen and City-sword, were a part of the congregation. This sight had the more weight with him, as by good luck not above two of that venerable body were fallen asleep.

This discourse held us till we came to the Tower; for our first visit was to the lions. My friend, who had a great deal of talk with their keeper, enquired very much after their health; and whether none of them had fallen sick upon the taking of Perth, and the flight of the Pretender? and hearing they were never better in their lives, I found he was extremely startled: for he had learned from his cradle, that the lions in the Tower were the judges of the title of our British kings, and always sympathised with our sovereigns.

After having here satisfied our curiosity, we repaired to the monument, where my fellow-traveller being a well-breathed man, mounted the ascent with much speed and activity. I was forced to halt so often, in this perpendicular march, that upon my joining him on the top of the pillar, I found he had counted all the steeples and towers which were discernible from this advantageous situation, and was endeavouring to compute the numbers of acres they stood upon. We were both of us very well pleased with this part of the prospect; but I found he cast an evil eye upon several ware-houses and other buildings that looked like barns, and seemed capable of receiving great multitudes of people. His heart misgave him that these were so many meeting-houses; but, upon communicating his suspicions to me, I soon made him easy in this particular.

We then turned our eyes upon the river, which gave me an occasion to inspire him with some favourable thoughts of trade and merchandize, that had filled the Thames with such crowds of ships, and covered the shore with such swarms of people.

We

We descended very leisurely, my friend being careful to count the steps, which he registered in a blank leaf of his new almanack. Upon our coming to the bottom, observing an English inscription upon the basis, he read it over several times; and told me he could scarcely believe his own eyes; for that he had often heard from an old attorney who lived near him in the country, that it was the Presbyterians who burned down the city; whereas, says he, this pillar positively asserts in so many words, that the burning of this ancient city was begun and carried on by the treachery and malice of the Popish faction, in order to their carrying on their horrid plot for extirpating the Protestant religion and old English liberty, and introducing Popery and slavery. This account, which he looked upon as more authentic than if it had been in print, I found, made a very great impression upon him.

We now took coach again, and made the best of our way to the Royal-Exchange, though I found he did not much care to venture himself into the throng of that place; for he told me he had heard they were, generally speaking, republicans, and was afraid of having his pocket picked among them. But he soon conceived a better opinion of them, when he spied the statue of king Charles the Second standing up in the middle of the crowd, and most of the kings in Baker's Chronicle, ranged in order over their heads; from whence he very justly concluded, that an anti-monarchical assembly could never chuse such a place to meet in once a day.

To continue this good disposition in my friend, after a short stay at Stock's-market, we drove away for the Mews, where he was not a little edified with the sight of those fine sets of horses which have been brought over from Hanover, and with the care that is taken of them. He made many good remarks upon this occasion, and was so pleased with his company, that I had much ado to get him out of the stable.

In our progress to St. James's-Park (for that was the end of our journey,) he took notice, with great satisfaction, that contrary to his intelligence in the country, the shops were all open and full of business; that the soldiers walked civilly in the streets; that clergymen, instead of being affronted, had generally the wall given them, and that he had heard the bells ring to prayers from morning to night in every part of the town or other.

As he was full of these honest reflections, it happened very luckily for us, that one of the king's coaches passed by with the three young princesses in it, whom by an accidental stop we had an oppottunity of surveying for some time: my friend was ravished with the beauty, innocency and sweetness, that appeared in all their faces. He declared several times, that they were the finest children he had ever seen in all his life; and assured me that, before this sight, if any one had told him it had been possible for three such pretty children to have been born out of England, he should never have believed them.

We

We were now walking together in the Park; and as it is usual for men who are naturally warm and heady, to be transported with the greatest flush of good-nature, when they are once sweetened; he owned to me very frankly, he had been much imposed upon by those false accounts of things he had heard in the country; and that he would make it his business upon his return thither to set his neighbours right, and give them a more just notion of the present state of affairs.

What confirmed my friend in this excellent temper of mind and gave him an inexpressible satisfaction, was a message he received as we were walking together, from the prisoner, for whom he had given his testimony in his late trial. This person having been condemned for his part in the late rebellion, sent him word, that his Majesty had been graciously pleased to reprieve him with several of his friends, in order as it was thought to give them their lives; and that he hoped before he went out of town they should have a cheerful meeting, and drink health and prosperity to king George.

ARTICLE II.

To the Editor of the Repository, *containing various political, philosophical, literary and miscellaneous articles, Vol.* II. *Page* 2. *Printed in London, January* 1789.

SIR,

THE papers accompanying this were written, and in part printed, with a view to appear in another place, but certain considerations have intervened to prevent the fulfilment of that intention. You will evidently see that they are too large for a newspaper and too small for a pamphlet. The long and very masterly letter you republished respecting the clergy in *Ireland* under the signature of "A SON OF THE CLERGY," (See Rep. Vol. I. page 459.) contains matter so analogous to that under discussion here, that you probably will not refuse to give place to the papers now sent you, merely because they bring a part of the same topics *home* to ourselves. Besides, I am encouraged to offer them to you from finding your work favourable to universal toleration and philanthropy. Under this impression, I remain, Sir,

Your well wisher,

A LETTER to a FRIEND, respecting the Debate in the House of Commons on Mr. Beaufoy's Motion in 1787, on the Subject of the Test Laws, as affecting the Dissenters: with Hints concerning the established Clergy, the Roman Catholics, the Jews, the Marriage Service, and other Topics touching the Church Establishment, and the State of religious Liberty in England *.

MY DEAR SIR,

YOU are pleased to ask my opinion of the arguments used, and of the vote passed in the House of Commons, on the 28th of March, 1787, when Mr. Beaufoy moved for a committee to consider of the test laws respecting the protestant dissenters. You will forgive me, if, in replying to you, I venture upon other topics.

The repulse experienced by the dissenters, from the vote of that day, ought not, I think, to discourage them from renewing their application. More apology is necessary from the dissenters, when they acquiesce in the restraints imposed upon them, than when they apply for their removal. They owe their best exertions, not only to themselves, but to the cause of liberty; they have to assert a right, and not to ask a favour; they have already lost much time, and they ought to lose no more. After the experience of a century, they may be convinced that they have nothing to expect from humility, and must owe their freedom to their importunity. By constant applications to the legislature, they are more likely to meet a conjuncture of circumstances favourable to their success, than by remaining inactive. I am apprehensive besides, that the ease which politicians have found in temporising with the dissenters, has induced a persuasion, that it is the only policy necessary to be employed with them; and therefore it is indispensable to prove, not only that the dissenters can no longer be duped, but that, being determined to persevere without ceasing, the shortest mode is to do them justice at once.

With respect to ministers of state, various circumstances may occasion a fluctuation, not only in their power, but in their opinions. If they are favourable to the dissenters, no arguments are necessary to invite their concurrence: if unfavourable, there is no reason for being deterred by their opposition.

If it be true, that the dissenters are embarked in a right cause, these seem proper observations.—Let us examine, then, whether any thing has occurred in this debate, upon Mr. Beaufoy's motion, to shew the dissenters in the wrong.—Not having been present at that debate, I must use the printed accounts of it, though without depending upon them so far as to refer any argument to any particular speaker, the discussion not being personal.

* A few of the considerations which appear in this letter have been made public before; but they have since been suppressed, to give place to the letter here published. ---The author will not be accused of plagiarism by the party most concerned.

The

The adversaries of the dissenters, I think I may affirm, have been challenged in debate; and though the history, and still more the present principles of the dissenters, lay fully open to their scrutiny, no arguments appeared drawn from either, whether upon the footing of right or of expediency, to invalidate their claims.

On the question of *right*, it was stated hypothetically, that cases *might* occur where the state might justly exclude persons from political power; but it was not proved that the protestant dissenters were persons of a description so to be excluded. It was next contended, negatively, that the exclusion of dissenters from offices, violated no right, because it inflicted no punishment, and did to them only what was done in other cases to other classes of men; which was saying, in different words, that the terrible incapacitations and penalties which attach upon dissenters when assuming their political rights, amounted to no punishment; and that a wrong might cease to be a wrong, when the instances of it were multiplied. No person can deliberately justify a third position which was advanced, namely, that because the church had *some* opponents, a bulwark should be raised against *every* sectary; consequently nothing will be offered here to refute a position so little guarded.

The adversaries of the dissenters seem to have obtained as little advantage in the debate on the topic of *expediency*, as on that of right. They maintained it to be inexpedient to deprive the legislature of a discretionary power over the dissenters, as if a *legislature* (ex vi termini) was not always competent to reassume this power when the occasion really called for it. They stated it likewise to be inexpedient by any concessions to alarm the church, which was allied by the tie of expediency to the state:—but they did not notice how much more reason there was to be dissatisfied with a clergy, capable of entertaining such puerile and uncharitable alarms: they did not advert to the impropriety of allowing the clergy to legislate for the state, which this doctrine implied, but which history has always shewn to be the source of fatal evil: nor did they recollect how easily the clergy in this country have had their alarms on this subject softened by time or conviction, or the fear of differing with the state on which it has so much depending.

The *general* arguments used by the opponents of the dissenters, seem not to have been better founded than those respecting the doctrines of right and expediency. To refer to the declining numbers and zeal of the dissenters, as a pledge for their innocent conduct, was called speculation; yet speculative representations were used in various instances *against* the dissenters; particularly when it was stated as necessary to guard, by exclusive laws, an ancient establishment, supported by a prodigious majority of the nation,

nation, against innovations from a few dissenters, capable only of acting through the medium of the legislature itself.

The supposition that, if the test laws were repealed, the dissenters might draw into their hands the several city and borough corporations, and thence taint our legislature, seems, in every view, overstrained. The third legislative branch is not in any extensive degree necessarily dependent upon corporations; and should any danger ever threaten from that quarter, there are wholesome remedies applicable to the evil. But the dissenters have neither power, nor concert, nor zeal enough, nor sufficient motives to induce them, to entertain a project so suspicious in its appearance, and so difficult and extensive in its execution, as that of obtaining a specific ascendancy in each corporation through the kingdom. To prove this, we have only to remark, that the dissenters, where they have most power, have seldom procured the return of dissenters to parliament; and that their candidates generally act as peaceable a part when chosen, as those returned by other descriptions of electors; and it is the use, rather than the extent of power, it is fact, rather than fear, which should govern the conduct of statesmen in the controul of rights. But, certainly, it was viewing a large question very partially, when the act respecting corporation offices was treated as the great grievance of the dissenters, who are equally debarred access to every public office whatever.

It was, farther, held as matter of necessity, for the state to look forwards, to guard the provision of the church. The dissenters, however, have not chosen to object to this provision. The landed interest, indeed, (in which the dissenters scarcely appear) has contended against the payment of tythes. But I presume the clergy will not urge the necessity of a test law, applicable to this question, being imposed upon the landed interest; though it would be more fitting for them, than for the dissenters, who rather make part of the monied interest.

That the dissenters have prayed for a release from the sacramental test, without proposing any substitute to it, was a remark true indeed, but without consequence. The dissenters do not oppose *civil* tests and *civil* qualifications, which embrace subjects of all religions and classes indiscriminately, and which are therefore unlikely to be burthensome to any; but they object to a *religious* test meant to exact a proof of conformity to an established church, and to secure objects which are by no means of political and temporal concern. A test, even of a civil nature, applied to sectaries purely on account of their religious tenets, without a pretence of their being objects for civil suspicion, would deserve reprobation, were it only from its fixing an unprovoked and unauthorised stigma upon their fidelity. In

In favour of the quieting effect of the prohibitory laws, the experience of a century was more than once appealed to. But the proof was certainly negative, and might just as well serve to shew these laws to have been *useless*, as *useful*. If experience is to be referred to, let the conduct of the dissenters *out* of office during the past century be well considered; let it be remembered, that, though the very laws in question made them outcasts from the political departments of society, they knew no waverings, either in times of rebellion or revolution, when many of the children of the church, within the pale of political liberty, had proved apostate; that they chose their part always, to a man; and that their exertions in favour of the constitution and Hanover succession, might always be relied upon, with the utmost certainty, whenever called for.

Merit was still more unjustly assumed in favour of the test laws, from the past harmony of the church. What reason is there, in the nature of things, for the clergy to run into discord, because dissenters are admitted into *civil offices?* Why must the clergy behave ill because the state does justice to others? But is not the harmony of the state much more important than the harmony of the clergy one among another? and is it not better that many should be in the right in the church, as to the doctrine of toleration, than that the whole church should be in the wrong? In short, experience shews that it is not difference in religious opinions which occasions discord, but rather the pretensions of one religious party to be paramount over another.

It was singular to hear the dissenters on one side contending, that the clergy ought to be enabled to obey with safety the rules of the church, by having it in their option to withhold the Sacrament from an unworthy communicant; and, on the other side, to find, that the clergy had disclaimed this indulgence, though it was stated to be criminal for them to refuse the Sacrament when called for as a civil qualification. Both our clergy, and their political friends, upon this occasion, must be presumed to treat very lightly those rules of the church, which, in other cases, they affect so strenuously to maintain.—But I mention the circumstance for the sake of a much more important observation. If it would be criminal to withhold the Sacrament from one desiring it as a qualification to serve his country, is it not criminal to place difficulties in the way of the *consciences* of other subjects, which oblige them of *themselves* to forego their means of serving their country? If Mr. Pitt, and his illustrious father, had been bred strict dissenters, would not their bosoms have burned within them, to think that this innocent circumstance, which might serve to prove their worth, must have doomed their public talents to languish inactive and unknown? What would France have done without a

Condé or a Turenne, without a Saxe or a Necker, if their public services had been stifled by a Test? Were not Newton and Locke sectaries in every thing but the name?

There was stress laid on one argument, which merits particular attention: It was said, that the king submitted to a Test. It belongs to others to shew, whether this Test is rightly or wrongly imposed; it is only necessary for the dissenters to prove, that the case of the king is different from theirs. The king, then, is not only a civil, but an ecclesiastical personage, and takes a Test as *head of the church*. He arrives at his civil and ecclesiastical offices, not by election or appointment, but by hereditary succession, and consequently without undergoing any previous enquiry. A deviation in his person from the principles of the majority of the nation, might occasion civil wars and commotions, and many inconveniences: since, by his appointment, all the great offices of the country are filled, whether ecclesiastical, judicial, military, or civil; and in him rests the power of peace and war, of forming alliances and treaties, of giving a negative to the proceedings of the two other branches of the legislature, and of modelling one of those branches.—Can the case of the king, then, be resembled to that of a dissenter applying to serve as a tide-waiter, an alderman, or even a secretary of state?

But a parallel of a different kind was attempted in the debate, the Sacramental Test being put upon a footing with an oath.—Let us compare the cases minutely.—An oath has civil objects in view; the Sacramental Test, ecclesiastical ones. The state has a right to search after evidence, and to obtain a promise of discharge of duties, which are undertaken towards it; but not to know the creeds of men. The oath being founded on a truth fundamental in all religions, is distinctive of none; while a religious Test supposes the profession of a specific faith. There is some toleration used as to the modes of administering the former; but the Sacramental Test, must only be taken in one mode. The oath only calls for that frame of mind which persons of good intentions may always possess; but it is held otherwise by many as to the communion at the Lord's table. The oath is effective, for its calls upon God to be a witness and avenger; the other is declarative only, and irrelative to the occasion for demanding it. The one is understood to be countenanced by revealed religion; the other, as a Test, has no precedent in the Bible or among men, being peculiar to this nation. The oath has even additional sanctions, namely, the public concurrence and opinion, and a personal sense of the propriety of the occasion for demanding it: while the Sacrament, as a civil test, derives efficacy upon the mind of the sectary from no external

ternal consideration whatever.—Under all these circumstances, * many good men have doubted the propriety of administering oaths in the manner usually practised; and shall the case of an oath, then, be paralelled to that of a religious Test?

The Test laws, it is said, however, do not oblige sectaries to take the Sacrament.—No, but they invite them to receive it criminally, and to " eat and drink damnation to themselves."—They rain snares upon men, and deliver them (contrary to our Saviour's prayer) into temptation. They corrupt the *moral* character of the sectary, for which no newly-adopted creed or ceremony can compensate, either to the individual or the state. And they do all this in a case where men have no right to impose any conditions of a religious nature.

It was indeed, maintained in debate, that Legislatures are impowered to propose Tests: but it should have been added, that these must be *civil* Tests.—Governments being commonly founded in force or ignorance, their first principles have been so little understood, that it is proper to give a reason for this limitation.—Men being by nature equal, an enlightened compact *ought* to be the basis of all government; and to say that there is actually no such compact, is only proving that governments have not yet been fairly constituted; and that upon a sufficient grievance or emergency, a compact may be reverted to.—Are religious rights, then, among those which men *would* give up in case of a compact? Are they such as they *could* give up? Are they such as they *ought* to give up? If these questions are answered in the negative, it is clear that government cannot exercise a right, which their constituents had neither inclination, power, nor obligation to invest in them.—It would be easy to dilate here; but I rather hasten to a conclusion of these comments.

A distinction in the debate was next attempted between legislative and executive offices, in order to do away the solecism, of dissenters being allowed to make, but not to execute laws; for it was said or implied, that the *people* elected persons to legislative, but not to executive situations. But this distinction is not founded. The lords (lay and spiritual) derive none of their legislative rights from popular election; and many corporate and other executive situations (as in hospitals, where the test laws apply in case of public endowment) are derived from popular election only. The solecism then exists: a dissenter may contribute to change every law in the land, even the test laws and those upholding the establishment, and yet cannot be made a sub-

---

* See more circumstances of this sort stated by Bishop Hoadly in his reply to Bishop Sherlock.

altern in a corporation: And he may plead as a counsellor in all courts of justice, as to the interpretation of laws, and yet cannot become a tipstaff in their menial execution.

Such were the argumentative objections to the claims of the dissenters, brought forwards by Mr. Beaufoy's motion. The protestant dissenters therefore, are under obligation to the abilities and information of the speakers on both sides;—to their friends, for shewing what may be said in their favour; and to their opponents, for proving how little some of the first talents in the country are capable of refuting their assertions.

There is one passage more (for I am particularly informed as to the fact) in the debate of 1788, respecting the protestant dissenters, which calls for pointed remark, and leads to some general discussion.—Mr. Pitt avowed to the legislature, that the bishops had thrown a powerful obstacle in the way of the dissenters, by declaring themselves *alarmed* upon the subject of their application. The bench of bishops has many respectable persons seated upon it, and some of them are even liberal towards sectaries; but their *esprit de corps* makes them afraid of differing from one another; and, having hitherto prospered so well, they are apprehensive of changes. It is nevertheless singular that the clergy should think to remain the same, when circumstances are no longer the same; *Idem manebat, neque idem decebat.* Perhaps they doubt of this fact, of a change of circumstances. They must however allow, that theirs is an empire of *opinion* only; and it can be no secret, that many able laymen having recovered from their blindness respecting the English clergy, are now lending the use of their eyes to many more. These then conceive the established clergy to be cooled in zeal and relaxed in manners; that their benefices are too frequently considered as sinecures; that their neglected schools and universities, far from supporting their antient reputation abroad, have driven our gentry at home into systems of private or of foreign education; that instead of useful or religious works, the clergy chiefly excel in works of taste, and that even of these the instances are few, compared with their numbers; that there is matter for censure both in the collection and in the partition of their revenues; that their boasted alliance with the *State* is commonly an interested alliance with the *minister*; with various other circumstances, which whether true or otherwise, make the impression of truth; and as they insensibly accumulate wait but for an occasion to break forth.—In such a situation, the clergy one should conceive, ought to conciliate those with whom they have any differences, instead of irritating them. They should wisely keep pace with the operations of time, instead of
confirming

confirming oppreſſions becauſe of their antiquity *. They ſhould even embrace any particular moment of power, as the fitteſt moment for conceſſion; not only to obtain the credit of moderation and generoſity, but to be able to preſcribe the meaſure of the conceſſion, and prevent its being productive of conſequences not intended. Their ſceptre is ſo viſibly departing from them, and they are under ſuch dependence on the crown and gentry for their beneficer, that (whatever miniſterial attentions they may have lately experienced) a prudent and powerful adminiſtration, and ſtill more the public itſelf, may controul them in many important reſpects. The very indifference ſhewn by the public to the late claim of the proteſtant diſſenters for liberty of conſcience, however ſatisfactorily viewed by the clergy, is in reality one of their worſt prognoſtics, indifference being the prelude to change.—The clergy conſequently appear rather to depend upon the ſtate, than the ſtate upon the good will of the clergy. —Since the clergy then have loſt ſo much in opinion, it is natural to aſk; whether they act wiſely in ſeeking a remedy for this loſs in the force of our habits, rather than in their own *popularity*; whether they ſhould not truſt to general eſteem, rather than to national prejudices; whether their conduct will not be better guided upon principles of preſent wiſdom, than of paſt power.

But it is proper for both parties to ſee preciſely what agitated the biſhops, when they preſſed their alarms upon Mr. Pitt?—Simply, the propoſition of reſtoring to their remaining executive political rights a handful of ſectaries, who have proved their attachment to their country, its conſtitution, and the reigning family; and who for a century have chearfully paid their contributions, not only to ſupport civil but eccleſiaſtical departments, though ſharing in the emoluments of neither.— This certainly was a ſtate and not a *clerical* queſtion; a queſtion of juſtice, and not of religion: and yet the clergy, who are told by their great but modeſt teacher, that their religion is not of this world, avowedly interfered in the things thus belonging to Cæſar.—It is ſingular that the laity did not take umbrage at this interpoſition of the prelacy, which favoured of proud catholic or narrow puritanical times. The clergy, having themſelves acquired an eſtabliſhment, were unreaſonable not to per-

* 'Surely every *medicine* is an innovation; and he that will not apply new remedies, muſt expect new evils; for time is the greateſt *innovator*. And if time of courſe alter things to the worſe, and wiſdom and counſel ſhall not alter them to the better; what ſhall be the end?' 'Time ſtandeth not ſtill, but contrarywiſe moveth ſo round, that a froward retention of cuſtom is as turbulent a thing as an *innovation*, and they that reverence too much old times, are but a ſcorn to the new.'— *Lord Bacon's Eſſays*.

mit

mit others to receive an unequivocal and unqualified toleration; being themselves *protestants*, with respect to the church of Rome, it was natural to expect they would allow of *dissenters* from themselves; and professing as they do, to be a spiritual and catholic church, they acted inconsistently in pursuing a temporal and narrow conduct.—The French clergy lately in a similar situation, conducted themselves with much more policy as well as charity, than the English bishops: They approved of the liberty allowed by the edict of their king to the non-catholics of France; and their only contention was whether they had not the merit of first suggesting the measure to the civil power.

The single point in which the English clergy can at any time be affected, is their *temporal provision*, which is the material object of every church establishment; for whether men are eminent for their wisdom or their want of it, they should equally renounce the folly of seeking to establish *opinions*, which by nature ought to have leave to fluctuate.—A temporal provision for the clergy is sure to subsist from age to age †, being sanctioned as well by the common sense, as by the common feelings of mankind; the close " alliance " of religion with morals and education, and the obligation of paying liberally for their united support, being acknowledged by all men. The clergy may rest assured that the episcopalian laity are not likely to exonerate the dissenters of this country from a compliance with this obligation, in the manner now fixed by the English laws.—But were the dissenters, who now support the double burthen of contributing to their own and the established clergy, disposed to revolt at it, nothing would afford them a stronger motive, than seeing the clergy exact a maintenance for *their* religion from those, to whom they would deny the unconditional exercise of their *own*.—If the established clergy however incline to mix in state affairs, it should at least be in a manner conformable to worldly wisdom; and it cannot be concealed that at present both in this country and in Ireland, they have material temporal questions at stake; as well as that the dissenters have able pens at command to permit their mixing the discussion. Can it escape the notice of that sagacity for which the clergy are eminent in their personal concerns, that the dissenters, animated as they now are, will renew their

* The encroachments of foreign sovereigns on ecclesiastical property, affect the regular and not the secular clergy; for though they are dissolving the monasteries subject to them very rapidly, they appear to leave the property of the secular clergy untouched.—This is what Henry VIII. did in England, without daring to proceed farther; he took away monks, but left clergymen. In truth, the clergy in England have not a superabundant provision: It is indeed levied in an improvident manner, and portioned out unequally; but this concerns the nation and the clergy themselves, more than the dissenters.

application

application as often repulsed, and at every renewal of it will feel more and more inclined to scrutinize the conduct of the bishops, whom Mr. Pitt has *publicly confessed* to be their principal enemies? Will the clergy then, when they have neither interest, reputation, nor duty to incite them, persist in a sullen and wanton opposition to innocent and equitable claims?

But are sectaries the only objects of terror to the church? Do they think nothing of *professed* infidels, who sap the rock of faith on which the church is built? The conduct of these, however, is easily explained. As long as the clergy preach " peace and " good will among men," and allow that their " kingdom is not " of this world," their conduct will silence these infidels; while a haughty, persecuting, and monopolizing spirit, must render them implacable to the clergy, as well as multiply their numbers. Let the clergy be diligent among their flocks and attentive to educate their youth, without calling sectaries to account for what respects only the Deity; and they will cease to have any enemies. Let them persuade statesmen of the *utility of religion to society*, not only by arguments, but by practical proofs; and they will find statesmen capable enough of distinguishing between faith and convenience, and of giving firm support to many things in practice which they do not fully credit. A few wranglers and sophists may occur and cannot be prevented; these appear in politics, in science, and in every department; but as they will meet with no public support, they may be viewed with a generous pity or a tranquil contempt. Since the church then can no longer controul the civil powers, or suppress controversy, their policy must take a new ground: they must act according to what they *are*, instead of what they *have been*.

It is an unnecessary generosity in the church to feel alarmed for the fate of the state or of the true religion, in case of protestant dissenters being restored to their utmost rights.——The sectaries in question, considered as a *body*, have long ceased to be ambitious in politics; they are respectful and accommodating as subjects; and the frequent voluntary suspension of their claims for admission to civil offices, is a presumptive proof of their disinterestedness, and of their principles being public rather than personal*. In short, humble as may be their temper and situa-

---

* See for proofs of this, two elaborate and able works, written in the manner of good old times, the first of which is intitled, *A Vindication of the Principles and Character of the Presbyterians of Ireland addressed to the Bishop of Cloyne, in Answer to his Book intitled the present State of the Church in Ireland,* by Dr. *William Campbell, of Armagh,* 3d *Edition;* printed in *London,* for *Evans,* 1787. The second work is intitled, *The Rights of Protestant Dissenters to a complete Toleration asserted;* by *a Layman,* 2d *Edition, London,* 1789.

C

tion, they are not afraid of comparing their *political* conduct tried by any constitutional *test*, with that of the body of bishops.—Whatever be the complexion of their *religious* character, their religion, I must say when speaking to religious persons, respects another and a superior being; a being, who has ample means to fulfill his *own* wishes respecting the weak and erring creatures of his power. No serious believer, in short, should countenance persecution, till there is a criterion to point out who shall exercise it. The very *desire* to persecute, seems of itself a sufficient objection to the validity of the right; for it implies a temper in the claimant, so opposite to that of christianity, that it never can be christian*. The feeble arm of force only stifles opinions

* The following extracts are from Mr. Turgot.—'Jesus Christ reproved his apostles for wishing fire to descend from heaven upon the Samaritans: every instance of his life is distinguished by a trait of this spirit. He did not tell his disciples to implore the succour of princes in order to compel infidels, and to make use of human authority to bring souls to him; but he told them to let the tares grow among the wheat till the time of harvest, when the master himself will make the separation. He performed miracles to convince the mind and not enslave the body. When the apostles proposed to repel the soldiers who came to seize him, he answered, that a legion of angels would be ready at his command to exterminate his persecutors; but that his kingdom was not of this world. He wrought a miracle to teach them not to confound the rights of God and those of Cæsar, things of heaven with things of the earth.—When he bids them invite all men to the marriage supper of the king, strong as the expression may be, it merely implied the degree of zeal with which his ministers ought to be inspired. *Compel them to come in*, said he, and as a proof that he did not mean to say *constrain them*, the guests at all times had the power of refusing, and others were invited in their stead. When his apostles themselves were about to forsake him, he merely addresses to them these affectionate words, *And will ye also go away.*

'He demands not so much external homage, as the sacrifice of the heart and attachment of the mind. An assent yielded through fear or interest, cannot make a christian; to be a christian, it is necessary to believe. Authority may indeed extort a sacrifice, but it cannot persuade. This therefore is not the method which Jesus Christ has ordained for propagating his religion. He has even excluded the penalties which the Jewish law enjoined against the disobedient: The prodigal son who leaves his father's house, is not pursued to deter others; his return is wished for, but it is not precipitated.

'Such is the spirit of the gospel. In the mean time I should be diffident of myself, and apprehensive of misconception, if I did not find the same sentiments in the fathers.—We shall be surprized at the warmth with which the founders of our religion preach this very doctrine of toleration, so contrary to the ideas of some men who are little informed upon the subject.' He then cites many of the fathers with great aptness and force.

The following passage is added in a note, 'The law of the Jewish religion can form no objection against toleration. God was the king of that nation: religion therefore was necessarily blended with the state; to violate the law was to be guilty of treason. Besides their laws, like the laws of a monastery, did not extend beyond the persons immediately under their jurisdiction. The Jewish religion moreover was very tolerant in regard to opinions purely speculative: Even the Sadduces who denied the resurrection of the body were not excepted from toleration.' See the Repository, Vol. I. p. 216-7.

in

in one country and age to reproduce them in another; it persecutes truth and error alternately; it generates hypocrisy; it obtains unanimity merely where it introduces ignorance; and when it has done its utmost, the virtuous life and the patient sufferings of a despised sectary often suddenly wrest from it all its converts.—Religions, in short, have usually consisted either in ceremonies, in morals, or in creeds; but ceremonies are too unmeaning and arbitrary to be taught at the expence of blood, excesses in morals will be guarded against by the civil power, while creeds respect only a private intercourse between God and man. How impious and impertinent is it for strangers to usurp a cognizance of the latter: how ridiculous to dictate forms to faith: how unjust to let the capricious dogmas of a part of a society prevail over the rights of the whole? Vain mortals, may we say to these religious pretenders, your reason fails you in your worldly concerns, and you think it infallible in the concerns of God; you mistake what you see, and you think yourselves right in what you cannot see; you will interpret, and you err! The radiant sun of heaven shines on the just and on the unjust, and dare you attempt to discriminate between men on earth on the part of the great creator; you, who know not whether yourselves are approved by him! Persecution, whether of a positive or of a negative nature, is persecution; for men are injured not only when they suffer evil, but when they are deprived of advantages. Let it then cease from the face of the earth; for in whatever shape it appears, it is unauthorised, it is needless, it is impolitic, and it corrupts all who resort to it.—This language may naturally be held to conscientious men.

It is worth adverting however to the different grounds on which persecution, in this country, has actually at different periods created or supported its power.—Our division of the Western church, remote from the sophistry of Greeks and Africans and from the fanciful tenets of oriental nations, long continued to possess that uniformity of opinion, which is the usual result of retirement and of ignorance; and found few, besides Jews and Mahomedans, against whom it could exercise its zeal. The clergy in the mean time, acquired a sway in the nation, exceeding that of its legitimate sovereigns, some of whom it even persecuted.—Little disposed as the nation had appeared to religious novelties, the alarm which had spread through Germany and the low countries at popish and monastic abuses, at last seized upon this island, and produced it in a succession of sectaries. The clergy on the one hand who had punished princes, were little inclined to spare subjects; and on the other hand, the sovereign power long accustomed to religious prejudices and so despotic habits, had no difficulty in seconding the wishes of the clergy. Thus the catholic reigns were spent in torturing the protestants, and the protestants reigns in oppressing other sectaries, who again in a moment of power found their means of retaliation; for persecution being a general principle in which all parties then joined issue, success alone decided who should be the victims of it.—Happily the foreign princes, who for the last century have swayed the screptre of this empire, having judged it prudent to cultivate the dissenters, the doctrine of *no bishop no king, no crosier no crown*, which had amused the Stuarts, long ceased to have countenance at court. The clergy therefore, appealing to the nation at large, which was still in the habit of intolerance, proclaimed the church in danger, pretending that if sectaries were legally tolerated, it must lead to the return of popery, of which every one stood in fear. But by degrees the dread of popery subsiding, liberal sentiments disseminating, religious zeal declining, and the reigning family becoming more secure, and therefore less in need of the aid of those revolution principles which had seated it upon the throne; the church solicited the aid of the civil power, under the new pretence of being its *temporal and political ally*.—For the honour of this country, however, many of the present episcopial clergy and laity not only consider *religious* motives for persecution as altogether obsolete; but treating the *whole* question as political, they are now beginning to ask, why religious topics should at all be held as *matter of public cognizance*, either by church or by state: they try the question upon political principles alone, and thence naturally find that neither church nor state has any right to interpose*.—I mean to convey no reflection on the present clergy from this *history*, since it is certain that the clergy of the present day are greatly softened in their sentiments: But it is right to endeavour to accelerate their complete reform, and to lead them to *act* upon sentiments which they cannot but begin to approve, if their professions are sincere.

Before I proceed to other matters, there are two or three arguments, which as they are disinterested in their origin, and have still an influence over many worthy minds, require to be obviated, as supporting the last dying sparks of persecuting zeal.——The first is, that the persecutor contributes to God's glory, by increasing the number of the orthodox and diminishing that of heretics. It is needless to re-argue the impropriety of men inter-meddling in what solely respects the deity, as well as the mistaken tendency of persecution: We can answer the argument much more shortly. Suppose an hundred forms of religion to prevail in the world, of which *one* only is the true; is it not

* See for example, Archdeacon Payley's works.

evident

evident that the doctrine of persecution, if generally established, would lead to the commission of ninety nine mischiefs, for one act of service that it performed: for how shall we limit the exercise of persecution, when every one will assert himself to be the supporter of truth? It is clear then, that we ought to propagate religion, as Christ did, by instruction and example: that we should persuade and not persecute; for the "wrath of man "worketh not the righteousness of God."—There is a second argument very much allied to this; namely, that none but the orthodox can be safe from punishment in another world: Thus charity to other men, becomes a pretext for persecuting them. Nothing however can be more hostile to the preceding consideration of God's glory, than the idea that one sect in this widely extended world can alone be saved. Many nations have never heard the glad tidings of the gospel: many individuals cannot read or enter into controversy; and yet many of these uninstructed persons are more virtuous than their persecutors. This doctrine then, by making the deity into a hard task-master, reduces us to the dilemma, either of denying the *divinity* of our religion, or the *goodness* of its author. Happily however this difficulty is altogether founded upon mistake: for God requires nothing from man beyond his best endeavours: He looks to intentions rather than to knowledge, to virtue rather than to speculation: He will not plunge men into misery for a few undesigned mistakes about the divine person, or attributes, or even commands: nor does he found his *glory* upon the misery of the majority of the human race.——Another argument that has misled honest men respecting persecution, regards not only the zealot, but the sceptic; it is, that all discussions respecting religious opinions, as leading to doubt and infidelity, must be carefully suppressed. The zealot has certainly little faith in his religion, who thinks that it can be shaken by controversy; or in providence, if he supposes that when so shaken, the deity if needful, cannot reveal to the human race fresh and convincing tokens of his will. I might as easily answer the sceptic, but I find I have been anticipated on this subject by the author of a late political work, whose words I have only to transcribe below*.

What

* 'There is a species of bigotry, peculiar in its nature, but frequent in practice 'belonging to certain sceptics, who are convinced of the use of religion to society, 'but fear that religious controversy may produce that want of faith in others 'which prevails in themselves. This position, being political, requires a political 'refutation which I think is to be found in the following observations.

'First, old established clergies (like other corporate bodies) usually fall into presumption 'and ignorance, and, when richly endowed, into idleness and vice, in proportion as they 'want opponents or rivals.

'Secondly, from clerical neglects and bad examples not only infidelity spontaneously 'arises in many, but is industriously propagated in others by infidel publications and 'discourses, intolerance itself being a sufficient motive with many for decrying a religion.

'Thirdly,

What above all, however, to be deprecated, is, the plan of regulating religion by political rules for political ends. I do not mean to argue respecting the impiety of this plan; for piety is seldom thought of in politics;—though I might observe (supposing religious arguments out of the question) that it is demonstrable, from civil and social considerations, that religious restraints are at least contrary to *natural and social rights*.—But it is necessary, as a man of the world to confine myself to the single point of utility, as certain divines have pretended, that both religion and ethics are adverse to our position. I contend, then, that it is evident in reason, and proved by experiment, that diversity in the forms of religion is necessary to meet the variety of sentiments naturally occurring in an age in which a system of general disquisition is established; that the species of religious faith and practice most conducive to political welfare, are eminently the offspring of choice; and that controul in religious cases, generates many political evils, and but few, and those very ambiguous, benefits. Statesmen may endow, if they please, any one profession of faith with wealth and honours; and they will find little opposition to

'Thirdly, Measures that are only imperfectly coercive, can scarcely prevent, and may sometimes increase religious disputes; as the toleration actually subsisting in civilized countries, of itself, permits considerable discussion; and the introduction of an entire restraint would be attended with various evils, more dangerous than any that could follow from the controversies meant to be extinguished.

'Fourthly, The systematic persecutors in question, more true to their feelings than to their theory, oftener seek to silence the disputes of Christians among each other, than to suppress the arguments of atheists and deists against religion in general: though it may be safely affirmed, in favour of European sects in general, that they have not only (their numbers and advantages considered) abounded in able defenders of religion, but have been particularly favourable to trade, manufactures, and sciences.

'Lastly, There is more aptitude to faith in the generality of mankind, than the timid theorists in question (arguing from their own example) may at first apprehend.—When we consider, therefore, that differences in opinion seem natural where men are allowed to think at all, and that persecution tends to produce either strife or lethargy; and when we add that toleration not only often affords an antidote to the decline of clerical manners, but admits the public strength to be augmented by the accession of numbers from every party; it will appear that we have, in these respects at least, a political compensation for any inconvenience arising from the mere extension of a tacit and imperfect, to an acknowledged and entire religious freedom (the difference between which is the whole matter here in contention in countries at all respectable for their civilization.)

'If Italy, Spain, and Portugal are compared with Great Britain, and with parts of Germany, Switzerland, and the United Provinces, we shall discover, that, wherever most bigotry and persecution prevail, religion is there worst vindicated, and, in many instances, is least respected; and political prosperity is there usually at its lowest ebb. On the other hand, in France we have had a proof of the possibility of statesmen manifesting more toleration even towards atheism, than towards protestant heresy.

'To conclude, the prejudice here combated does not, in any event, appear to require more than the suppression of public religious disputations, beyond which, therefore, its zeal ought not to be extended (supposing it proper to be indulged at all.)

'Let it be added, as a justification for the above remarks, that the practice of persecution has been so general, and its effects so terrible, that there is scarcely any country in Europe where it is not necessary to combat its remains.' Old and new Principles of Trade compared, p. 52.

it

it, if they leave others to their spontaneous exertions. But it is clearly the duty of politicians to strengthen the state, by the confidence, at least, of *all* parties; instead of confining it to the attachment of *one* party, whose confidence it obtains by paying for it, and whose advice is always to be suspected with regard to the rest, from its having erroneously taken up a persuasion that a state of hostility towards them is both meritorious, and for its own interest. No party, however large it may be, ought to be cultivated so exclusively, as to prevent a due comprehension and combination of the *whole* *.

But it is time to quit this general discussion, though, before I lose entire sight of the debate in 1787, I think it necessary to say some words respecting Mr. Pitt.—This minister, I am happy to find, did not (and how is it possible, educated as he has been, that he should) argue against the protestant dissenters on the ground of general principles. He took the ground of *expediency* only; and, as expediency changes from day to day, his conduct may easily change. This may afford some consolation to the dissenters for his late opposition.—But no talents, however intuitive, can supply the want of experience; which, considering the sparing manner in which instruction arises out of different scenes at different times, must, by the laws of nature, necessarily be the reward of age, and of extensive converse with men in different countries. To an experience of this sort, accompanied with parts and celebrity in nothing inferior to those Mr. Pitt, we owe the following observation respecting sectaries, which I recommend to that gentleman's consideration. ' Remember me affectionately,' says the venerable person to whom I allude, in one of his familiar letters, ' to the ' honest heretic ***. I do not call him *honest* by way of distinc-
' tion; for I think all the heretics I have known have been
' virtuous men; they have the virtue of fortitude, or they would
' not venture to own their heresy; and they cannot afford to be
' deficient in any of the other virtues, as they would give advan-
' tage to their many enemies, and they have not, like orthodox
' sinners, such a number of friends to excuse or justify them.—Do
' not, however, mistake me. It is not to my good friend's heresy
' that I impute his honesty: on the contrary, it is his honesty
' that has brought upon him the character of heretic *.'—Perhaps
this

---

* I mean, in a separate letter, to consider at length Bishop Warburton's work on the alliance of the (established) church and state, on account of the deference presumed to be still paid to it by churchmen and statesmen, and to attempt to shew, chiefly by means of a plain analysis of it, that it is a tissue of sophistry, and unworthy of being treated as a book of any authority.

* ' I am inclined to attribute two positive advantages to our modern European sects:—
' First, there is a presumption (as morals happily bear a connection with almost every
' scheme of religion existing in modern times in Europe) that, whenever the sense of
' religion is active enough to assume the form of a sect, a certain decency of manners will
accompany

this anonymous authority will not be convincing to Mr. Pitt. Let him then yield to authority and argument united in the words of his illustrious father, when replying in a debate in the House of Lords, to Archbishop Drummond, who had charged the dissenting Clergy with a *close ambition*. "After such proofs of honesty, (said "Lord Chatham) to suspect men of close ambition, is to judge "uncharitably; and whoever brings this charge against them "without proof, defames."—Here he made a short pause, and the eyes of all were turned on the Archbishop, who made no reply; Lord Chatham then repeated his words, and added: "The Dis-"senting Ministers are represented as men of close ambition; my "Lords, their ambition is to keep close to the college of fisher-"men, not of cardinals; and to the doctrine of inspired apostles, "not to the decrees of interested aspiring Bishops. They contend "for a spiritual creed, and scriptural worship; we, my Lords, "have a Calvinistical creed, a Popish liturgy, and an Arminian "clergy. The Reformation has laid the scriptures open to all; "let not the Bishops shut them again. Laws in support of "ecclesiastical power are pleaded for, which it would shock hu-"manity to execute. It is said that religious sects have done great "mischief where they are not kept under strict restraint: My "Lords, history affords no proof that sectaries have ever been "mischievous, when they were not oppressed and persecuted by "the ruling church."—These remarkable words, dictated by an enlarged and reflecting mind, are extracted from the printed relations of the time: but they need no voucher; they mark their great author, and enoble him to *all* posterity, I hope we shall not be left to say, with the exception of his *own*.

I am not enough acquainted with the protestant dissenters, to know their present sentiments on two topics, which may possibly soon come before us all for discussion. The first is that of the *Roman Catholics*.

Protestant dissenters have been in habits of dreading the Roman catholics, both on a civil and religious account. It is proper, however, for them to review this question, and to see whether the times have not changed, and men in them; and whether, forgetting the past, it is not both just and prudent rather to aid,

' accompany it in the mass of sectaries; and this expectation is rendered the more pro-
' bable, by the watchful eye usually kept by every party over the conduct of sectaries.—
' Secondly, when the sectary finds that he cannot himself become established, he natu-
' rally looks to self defence, and hence he commonly (at least in modern times, and when
' he is in danger of being oppressed by the establishment or the civil government) ends in
' being more or less an advocate for religious, and thence, probably, for a certain mea-
' sure of civil liberty; both of which are connected and beneficial political principles,
' and have a considerable effect in enlarging and giving vigour to the human character.
' If these rules, in favour of the existence of modern European sects, have their excep-
' tions, these exceptions seem likely to be but small and transitory.' Old and new Principles of Trade compared, p. 51.

than

than to obstruct, the applications which the Roman catholics are said to be meditating to the legislature for their own relief. I know that the Roman catholic creed is reputed to contain one or two doctrines repugnant to civil authority; but I know, at the same time, that the practice of men is often better than their creeds. Neither the catholics, nor dissenters, nor episcopalians of England, are to be judged of from our books of *history*; and the abominable spirit of a Gardiner and of a puritan, as well as of a Laud, have happily become obsolete: It is the British catholic (as well as protestant dissenter) of the *present day*, whose case is under examination. And here, we must confess that the erroneous prejudices of the British catholics are visibly abated; that the rapid decline or extermination of the Pope's authority in the most bigoted catholic countries, and the lessened influence of their clergy, are solid confirmations of the fact; that the Stuart race no longer affords even the shadow of a Popish pretender to the throne; that the catholics are ready to give every test that honour can offer, I will not say for checking their religion, but to prove their religion altered; and lastly, that their numbers are too inconsiderable to excite the smallest apprehension, especially when combined with their change of temper.—There is now in various countries happily grown up with time, a mass of evidence, proving that the Christian religion, in all its forms, is by its own nature peaceable; that its professors alone, by mixing it with civil concerns, have rendered it otherwise *; and that the widest charity of temper in nations, is attended not only with most peace, but with most knowledge, wealth, population, and power. If the civil doctrines, however, of the catholics, are still to be guarded against, it should certainly be by generous, civil, and not by narrow religious tests: And if the professions of attachment of a papist towards a supposed heretical government are held in their nature *felo de se* and nugatory, and if a catholic in no course of ages is supposed able of purging himself from the imputation of his ancestor's errors; let a *pecuniary security* be substituted for, or accompany, wherever

---

* 'I am conscious how many wars heresies have occasioned: but was it not because we were desirous of persecuting such? The man who believes with sincerity, believes also with more firmness, when you would oblige him to change his creed, without at the same time convincing him, and becomes obstinate: his obstinacy kindles his zeal, his zeal inflames him. You wished to make a convert, you have made a fanatic and a madman. Men ask nothing more for their opinions than freedom: if you would take it from them, you put arms into their hands, grant it them, they will remain tranquil, as do the Lutherans at Strasbourg.—It is then the unity of religion to which we would compel men, and not the multiplicity of opinions which we tolerate, that occasions commotions and civil wars. The Pagans tolerated every opinion, the Chinese do the same: Prussia excludes no sect, Holland includes all, and these nations have never experienced a religious war. England and France have wished to have but one religion, and London and Paris have seen the blood of their inhabitants flowing in streams.''— Expressions of M. Turgot, see Repository No. 4. p. 219.

requisite, the civil test.—As to a sacramental test imposed upon the catholics, especially taken upon the spur of a momentary occasioned, and not required retrospectively as an evidence of past conduct, it is still more nugatory than an oath can be supposed to be, and ought, on all accounts, to be given up.

In the present struggle for religious liberty, it would give me concern, not to find the *Jews* included; and this is the second topic to which I last referred.—Their religion is the mother of all the religions of Europe, of European America, and of a principal part of Asia and Africa; and should naturally experience kindness from all her children. Jealousy in the subject, rapacity in the sovereign, and bigotry in the priesthood, have rendered the Jews the objects of former persecutions; but shall we boast in the present day of civilization, and be wanting in humanity; or of taste and the fine arts, and be wanting in feeling; shall we know in short every thing but the rights of men? We have improved ourselves in words and in speculations only, if our temper is still uncharitable; we have dropped the savage without, and not the savage within, if we cannot live in peace with persons of all communions.—If there are any fair objections to the Jews, they are of a *civil* nature, and respect their manners; yet where their manners are censurable, it is chiefly to be attributed to their persecutors. A fuller participation in rights of society, must communicate to the Jews a fuller portion of its usual sentiments and manners. Sectaries are by nature given to zeal; and nothing operates upon men more than a kind government. Besides, the wealth and trading connections of the Jews are very considerable, while our merchants and other subjects are too firmly established to suffer by their rivalship.—What obstacle then is there to our offering without reserve, to this widely scattered nation, which has still a place in God's particular providence, an asylum from the severities they experience in foreign parts? Nothing less than actual misdemeanour in the Jews should bring them again into bondage; and an experiment only can enable us to pronounce upon this: for suspicion is here an insufficient ground for rigor, the innocence of men in religious cases being to be presumed upon, and by no means their guilt.—The protestant dissenters in particular ought not to be displeased with this language. They can find nothing in scripture which puts the Jews under any other tutelage or discipline, than that of providence: and in the rights of men, I am sure they cannot read their proscription. If I mistake not, one of the most valuable of the dissenting clergy (Dr. Price) has reprobated the term of toleration when applied to religious liberty; for it simply means suf-

ferance

ferance, and as the use of it is unknown with respect to civil liberty, it falsely implies that the claim to each has not an equal foundation.—When the protestant dissenters cease to be the friends of *universal religious liberty*, they forfeit one of their best distinctions; for those who care for themselves only, are but one degree removed from persecuting their neighbour.

I shall end with another short observation.—I have often wondered that a part of the English church service, imposed upon and submitted to by the whole English nation, the Quakers excepted, has never been objected to, till very lately*; I mean the marriage service.——It has many absurdities in it universally acknowledged, and is certainly one of the many unjust impositions made by human authority. Some formalities of a *civil* nature are requisite, on the occasion of marriage, for the purposes of civil society; and there can be no sufficient objection to the performance of them in a place so public, respectable, and convenient, as a church; or to the payment of the attendant fees to the clergy, as the persons who officiate in it considered as a civil occurrence. But if religion is intermixed in this transaction, the service ought at least to be made rational, and such as shall not offend sectaries, or conscientious men; or at least the submission to the religious part of the ceremony should be left optional to the parties.—I presume that the reason why the service, as it now stands, has been so long and generally received, not only by the protestant dissenters, (who at first were with little exception, occasional conformists to the church,) but by the nation at large; is, that no motive can be imputed to the persons complying with it that is of an improper nature; the object of marriage being as useful to the public, as desirable to individuals.—I point out the case however as an injustice, by the modification of which the clergy may obtain some credit, without any hazard either to themselves or to the remaining parts of the liturgy.

I am comforted for your sake and my own, my dear sir, at having thus concluded a letter which long as it is, might have been swelled with other matter. I have touched upon two new topics (respecting the Roman Catholics and Jews) concerning which the body of protestant dissenters have not of late I believe declared themselves; but I think at the same time, that the topics so started ought as soon as possible, to come before *them* and the *public* for serious consideration and discussion.—If the protestant dissenters

---

* See Dr. Priestly's letter to Mr. Pitt on Toleration, &c. 2d Ed. 1787. This celebrated controversialist and philosopher, whose opinions are generally as novel in theology as in philosophy, says good humouredly in behalf of his brethren, on this subject. "If we "were not taken, as it were, at an advantage, when we are disposed to make "light of small obstacles, we should certainly make loud remonstrances on the subject."

are selfish enough to feel adverse or indifferent upon them, they will lose much of the wishes of good persons in their favor. Men have frequently religion enough to induce them *to hate each other*; but it is clear that the Christian religion was revealed for a very different purpose, namely, that of making us *love even our enemies.*

If I have used any improper language in these pages, it is by mistake, and I will readily correct it when pointed out. I wish only that strong arguments and strong facts which I have a right to employ, may not be mistaken for strong expression, to the use of which I have no right, and which would only disgrace my subject and dishonor their author.

I am, my dear Sir,

Your's, &c.

ARTICLE III.

PREFACE, *by an* ENGLISH PROTESTANT, *to* JOHN PHYSIOPHILUS's *specimen of the Natural History of the various Orders of Monks, after the manner of the Linnæan System;* (*written by* BARON BORN,) *translated from the Latin, printed at Augsburgh.* London: *printed for Johnson.*

THE essay to which this is prefixed is considered as the production of Baron Born of Vienna, who has himself been signalized as one of those naturalists alluded to in the *author's* preface, and who is sufficiently known in England by the fine collection in natural history which he disposed of to the earl of Bute. The reader may be gratified to learn another circumstance, which is, that this satirical performance is thought to be patronized by the emperor of Germany; this satire in return facilitating, the enterprizes of that prince against the orders of monks.

In translating this book, no design is entertained of encouraging the *persecution of papists*, either in England, Scotland, Ireland, Canada, or America. God forbid that protestants should take up one of the most odious practices of papists; namely, that of interfering in their neighbour's private concerns with God Almighty!—And indeed the true religion would have a poor chance for an extensive increase, if force were the only medium of its propagation; as so many bad religions, and bad shapes of a good religion, have been beforehand with it in the four quarters of the world, of which Europe is by far the least. The true policy therefore for any religion capable of propagating *itself*, and destined for that end, is to engage the temporal powers always to stand *neuter* in religious contests. This would leave the passage for circulating a prevailing religion always open.

The best way of making converts of the papists in this country, is to induce them personally to regard us and so to mix with us, that the influence of society may shame them out of their tenets and practices, or at least out of the more absurd parts of them; which being done, we may safely leave them in possession of the other parts.—It is not popery that so particularly merits our aversion, as the species of papists that popery has usually produced; who, having been generally either abetted or oppressed by the temporal power, have been placed in the two situations which are of all others the most apt to engender passions destructive to those about them, and to their own character.—Indeed it is observable in those countries where the magistrate takes no party in religion, that protestants and papists are capable of living together in sufficient harmony.

Ridicule being a far more powerful engine for their genuine conversion than persecution (which by recent experience in the case of the emperor's protestant subjects in Hungary, is found rather to hide, than to change the minds of men;) this publication against monks and nuns may have its use at this singular period of revolutions.—And it is to be hoped that no pious person will be shocked with the gaiety of it. Monasteries and nunneries by no means form a part of the religion of Christ himself, or that of his early followers. They are not necessarily a part even of popery, any more than the inquisition is; since there are catholic countries, or at least parts of them, that are absolutely without either; and they are found among other sects whom papists would be ashamed to imitate.—They are also of no use in propagating the catholic religion; for sensible travellers know those countries to be often the least attached to their religion, that have the most provisions for being so; and if heretics were to be admitted among them of sufficient zeal and talents, they would immediately have many converts; the reasons for which will soon appear conspicuous.

Monks and nuns are often compared to drones among bees. The comparison is forcible, because it reminds us not only of all the articles in which they agree, but in which they differ. Drones agree with these animals in being idle; they agree in being buzzing, and having a disposition to thrust themselves into

every

every one's concerns, notwithstanding their idleness; they agree in being stupid; they agree in being fond of rifling the fairest growths of nature, and yet in being found in the most fetid places of retirement, covered with dust and cobwebs; they agree in producing no sweets for society, and yet in devouring the chief sweets of it; and they agree also (at least the more scrupulous religious agree,) in having their proper uses of sex extinguished.—In other points the comparison fails. Drones have no stings, while the religious are armed with the persecuting stings of hornets; and drones do not obstruct though they steal from the industry of their neighbours, while the religious act, in this respect, as opiates to society, in cases even where such industry might contribute to their own personal use.

There are many strong reasons to be urged, why the regular * Religious should be extirpated, even by papists themselves. A few only of these reasons shall be named.

The first is, that they lessen the labourers of society. In Spain, and other principal catholic countries, a few subjects only exert themselves, and charity (as it is called) makes it superfluous for the rest to do any thing besides humiliating themselves before the religious orders. Of course, such countries abound in idle beggars, want all manner of conveniencies, and have a despotic clergy.—Perhaps a worse objection to these orders, is, that they furnish too alluring a means to stifle a nation's activity, by providing for the younger branches of families; parents by this means losing a spur to industry in the providing for such, and the younger children themselves wanting their sphere for being industrious. It is chiefly to those very ranks, that are there cooped up in walls, ceremonies, and stupidity, that flourishing states owe their great movement and prosperity. In catholic countries, however, (where, by means of their connections, capitals of money, and capacity, they might lead the inferior people to labour, and induce the higher to protect them) they, in fact, tend to suppress all industry, and to introduce universally those opposite ideas, but consistent qualities, of pride and contented beggary; whence exertion not only becomes distasteful to the poor, to whom the contagion extends, but unsuccessful also with them, through their ignorance and helpless condition. The restoration, in such nations, of an intermediate order between the rich and poor, might be attended with the most brilliant and sudden good effects.—It is singular to observe another objection to these orders, which is, that almost all the bigotted catholic countries in which they are numerous, are full of libertinism; to say nothing of

---

* So called from following a "*rule*," the *rule* of their order.

more obscure or obscene vices, which one is not permitted to name, but which nevertheless immoderately abound. And how shall women be chaste, when their religious guides and censors (who have close and frequent access to them) become their very seducers? In these countries it is, that the younger clergy, upon principles of luxury, might object to a permission to marry; and if single young women are here often remarkably correct and reserved in their carriage, it must be noticed, that they are kept, during their youth, in the most unsuspecting ignorance, and are studiously watched by attendant friends.—When these mechanical restraints terminate, how often do we discover, in marriage, the intriguing matron, the varieties of whose favours, at least in the larger cities, generally prevent her progeny exceeding two or three children? This, however, is not the whole evil. No countries are more deficient in knowledge and arts, than those that are full of monks, unless powerful incidental causes intervene. Men, without rivals, and without liberality, grow indolent and opiniated, and, of course, make bitter enemies to those that aim at knowledge; the introduction of which, in others, would quickly extinguish that deference to themselves, whence spring their prodigious power and revenues. Thousands are the monasteries throughout Europe; yet Europe hardly knows one man of extensive reputation to be computed in each order, in each state, where they prevail.—Being unhappy and selfish, no wonder that these orders are ill-natured. We chain up brutes, by way of making them surly; and the experiment succeeds equally with man.

The same being that is acknowledged frail *without* the monastery, continues frail when shut up within it. Undertakings that are beyond the tone of human nature, must produce disgust or artifice; and, as religious novices are not always voluntary, or determined to the act by religious motives, or apprized of the whole sacrifice they are making, something of human nature must break forth again. A cell is a cell, and not a place of magic; and there it is that the fettered mind, at its moment of solitude, is reminded of passions in the flesh that remain unappeased, of the liberty and variety of action and of society from which it is cut off, and usually experiences its incapacity or scruples to serve heaven in the way it finds prescribed. With many of the religious, the chief of their worldly passions find their full indulgence under different forms; ambition being ambition though in a cloyster, and there being the same identity in their other passions and habits; such as pride and revenge, indolence or activity, jollity or luxury, attention to the arts or frivolous reading, or whatever may be the medium or object.—In short, there is too much that is human in man for it ever to be divine; and

still

still more so, where the institution for changing it is ill planned, and screened from public view.—As the greater part of those that adhere to the rules of their order *must* feel oppressed by its rules, (and those who do not adhere to them, ought not to be held as belonging to the order) these institutions are not to be considered as calculated for *earthly* happiness; and as little are they for *moral virtues*. Even chastity, which is the virtue chiefly affected, is so little attained, that loose manners and unnatural vices are the frequent substitutes for matrimonial happiness; which is not only *not* illicit in the eye of heaven, but (as we daily see) is connected with the most useful virtues, which parents have opportunities of inculcating through whole families of children.— Let that impiety, then, be silenced, which says, that public institutions so oppressive, delusive and destructive, can be at all necessary to heaven.

If an astronomer could draw an inhabitant out of the moon, and make him descend to be a near spectator of this world of ours, round which he has so often travelled, how singular must his prospect be in this particular!—A race of beings would discover itself, whom nature had divided into two parts or classes, purposely that they might have a progeny. A sect among them would be found, who deny this to be nature's plan, and affirm her to be best pleased with their separation, as the proper means of mortifying their carnal, and exalting their mental part. If the lunar visitant should ask for examples of this, he might be shewn the fat monk, ruddy with the meats and drinks and spoils of life, eluding, by a thousand stratagems, the destination of his founders; and, in the place of mental improvements, he might see large possessions and estates collected, fine buildings and gardens, political intrigues, and religious feuds, no arts encouraged that were not of the ornamental kind, no knowledge of God's works, but perpetual recourse to man's sophistry, and, in short, no benefits from these establishments not attainable in a thousand ways far more elegible and innocent.

If the astronomer should mount his guest a little higher, he might display to him those European countries most abounding in religious orders, as countries the most impoverished and despotic; and if he found a few exceptions, they would be owing to certain relics of trade, or to former wise establishments, or other incidents, of which the number of these institutions was rather the consequence than the cause.

But what must be the horror of a good tempered stranger, upon viewing smoke arising from the burning of a human victim at the altar of these Religious! " Why is it, cruel inquisitor, " that you torture thus one of God's subjects?"—" I am per- " suaded (he will answer) I am acting right."—His victim could
" reply,

"reply, I am persuaded of being right, alike with yourself."
"I will prove it by reasons," says the inquisitor.—"And could
I not prove it by reasons also," might the roasting victim reply, "think you that you would find me here your prey? Mind
your own affairs with your creator, and because I have minded mine with him, do not destroy the creator's works: I am
his being not your's. The God that suffers plants of two
kinds to grow upon the earth, the God that suffers animals
to be various, has made the mind of man various, and let us
each take our course. The best test that we can each urge for
ourselves is our self persuasion. The power of burning me
is accidental: In another country I might burn you. But
remember that under a *merciful* God, that system which is
cruel, must also be false."—Expostulations of this sort have
force with every body but an inquisitor or a monk.

But it is time to return to the best object of these remarks, which is, to show what are really those present *adjuncts of popery*, which popery may do without.—Can we see do without the regular clergy, such as *monks* and *nuns*. We must not use false arguments. Monasteries do not hurt population merely by keeping half a million of people from marrying, while so many millions are so ready to marry if they could find subsistance: They hurt population principally, by checking that activity which multiplies food. They hurt society by giving away the products of it to those who furnish no equivalents to serve for its farther accommodation; and they hurt it also by spreading bad manners, leaguing themselves with bad governments, and stifling the necessary rivalship and freedom in the sciences and arts. The same religious person who perhaps would almost worship a deceased *heathen* poet or comedian, will not permit a skilful countryman of his own to bake his bread, or mend his shoes, if a heretic; and yet would give away his wine and oil and corn to *foreign* heretics to gladen *their* hearts, and receive and use any of their commodities in return.—It would be impertinent however to suppose the regular clergy destitute of worthy members. But let it be remembered, that equal numbers of the same rank would naturally produce a proportion of valuable persons, if left to walk the world at large; and that whatever may be the merit of individuals, the leading features of their *societies*, are pride, ignorance and envy, luxury and rapacity, with a persecuting, turbulent, despotic spirit: their charity consisting chiefly in distributing about the fruits of the earth, which in protestant countries is equally well done by the means of sale and purchase; that is, by establishing a supply of conveniencies as the proper return for food, to the benefit of the whole.—Monkhood therefore is one of the articles which popery might safely discard.

It might discard also a part of the doctrine of the *pope's infallibility*. The Gallic church, the Venetians, and the chief of the powers of Europe, have fairly set this political weapon at defiance; and if the pope absolves any persons from sin among them, he no longer absolves them from temporal allegiance. It is incumbent therefore on all catholics who ask toleration of protestants, explicitly to banish from among themselves any remnant of this doctrine; for as allegiance to a foreign prince is repugnant to the ideas of all societies, it will always furnish a pretext for their *own* persecution.

It is diabolical to say, that faith is not to be kept with heretics; because even heretics are men, and moral truth is necessary for the peace and safety of *men*. Such positions are useful only in a moment of power: When the scene alters, injustice is found to be as much a *reciprocal* law, as justice itself.—In truth there are few papists who believe this infernal doctrine in its full extent, where any advantages for education subsist; which should induce the papist to disclaim a doctrine to which he probably does not give ear, and the protestant to allow education to every papist submitted to his power.

Celibacy in the secular clergy is another practice, that is not fundamental. Many papists have themselves thought this circumstance open to change, and it greatly imports the reputation of their clergy that a change should take place. Sons are relations quite as reputable as "*nephews*," and virtuous wives of their own, more decent than proselytes made of the wives of others. In this country we find that matrimony has not half the evil effect upon bishops that *preferment* has, to which no catholic bishop has ever yet objected.—In short, the great rule in human affairs is, to leave a vent to mortal passions, and not to ask too much from man.

The *inquisition* even by the confession of papists themselves, is not an indispensible ingredient in catholic practice. Let those who think so, suppose Christ living; and after picturing the parable of the good Samaritan of the house with *many mansions*, let them suppose him turning round and beholding a set of inquisitors marching towards a lighted pile. One cannot speak in the place of one inspired, but these would be the feelings of a disciple: The scene would remind him of Christ's own cross; the inquisitors would seem high priests and pharisees, and he would incline to throw the inquisitors upon the pile instead of the victims. Even Christ himself might say, "Inquisitors, I know you not."—How happy had man never known these wretches, who have introduced the fires of hell upon earth, and who though perhaps themselves among the worst of men, yet pretend to judge those whom God and Christ would pardon!

In short, when one contemplates the political, as well as the religious mischief that they introduce in a nation, one is inclined to think that they are as great a scourge to their own people, as to heresy itself.—The faggot however is only persecution in excess. Every oppression under pretence of religion is an act of inquisition, injurious to politics, and execrable before God and man. Can the Deity approve of persecution, when it fills the persecutor with crimes and passions, more odious than heresy itself?

There are various other particulars in the Romish religion like the foregoing, which it might surrender without injury to its essence. Papists themselves have in some cases been wise enough to discourage *holidays*; which, serving for nothing so little as devotion, and especially towards the prime divinity, should no longer be lost to profitable labour.

An *unknown tongue* necessarily implies an unknown religion, and this again an interpreting despotic priest; who is more fatal to human prosperity than a thousand heretics, by whom the peace of the *laity* is rarely disturbed, unless in consequence of their persecution. It were therefore to be wished that every state used its own translation of the bible.—The same remark applies to the language of the prayers of papists. At present the clergy conduct the whole dialogue in this religion: They interpret for the Divinity, and they interpret for man, and faithfully for neither. Can any thing however be more assuming?—Why did not Jehovah and Jesus speak heretofore in Latin, and why was there ever a gift of tongues, but for the plain reason, that *revelation* (by the very term of it) implies that it was meant to be *understood?* It seems that hieroglyphics and mystery first made their appearance among Ægyptian sorcerers; How natural then from this disguise of the Romish clergy, to suspect them, if not of sorcery, yet of a stupidity that fears the light. Perhaps this singular stratagem in the catholic religion of using an unknown tongue, is of all others the fittest for proving, that men may too easily be made back again into brutes, by the machinations of men.—" But beware, short-sighted priests, lest you become a
" prey to your own inventions. You understand nothing your-
" selves, merely in consequence of not suffering others to un-
" derstand. Remember, however, that your disciples are now
" walking by the rays of other lights, than *yours*. In your pre-
" sent state, you are expensive machines in society; and with-
" out you reform and become useful, laymen will learn one
" of two things, either to make you do with less mummery
" and expence, or employ others to serve them."

There is another particular which seems unnecessary to popery, because it is unnecessary to any religion; which is, *that of*
supposing

supposing itself the only *mode of salvation.* From this doctrine however originates that modest, tender care for one's neighbours, which leads a monk to cut the throats of those who seek any other line of salvation. But the Deity does not thus lay a trap for men: He did not make so many myriads of them, only to punish and destroy them: And the inhabitants of China, India, Turkey, and nineteen twentieths of the globe, may still be saved through virtues adapted to their state of knowledge, notwithstanding the papist is vain and cruel enough to think, that he alone can procure notice from the Almighty. From the darkness of many speculative doctrines, it is evident that the Deity wants pious practisers, rather than minute believers; and that he wishes us to have religion for *our* sakes, rather than his own. But at all events, the religion that teaches what is detestable, never can be divine; and even Christianity could not be divine, if it taught us to oppress mankind, in cases where the Deity did not dictate the instance for doing so in person. And least of all should *that* Christian venture to persecute his neighbour, who has not permission to read his own bible to learn what is taught in it. But it seems that those who understand their own concerns the least, are usually the most ready to invade the concerns of others.

Confessors are so immediately interwoven in the practice of popery, that a tone of caution must be observed with respect to them. It is not however to confession, and spirital reproof, and the like, that we can form objections; the only doubt is with respect to priestly flattery, and the power of pronouncing absolution by frail or ignorant men.

Any fundamental reform in the Catholic religion will certainly include the doctrines of *dispensation, human mediation,* and *works of supererogation*; since nothing can be more injurious to the purposes of morals, than that sinners should be excused from their basest vices and covered with foreign merits, by means of a paltry piece of money or legerdemain. Unfortunately the present Catholic religion, in order to secure to itself followers, accepts of *rites and amulets* instead of virtues: With a view to revenue, it makes compensation for sin *pecuniary:* From its present absurdities also, it is induced to encourage *stupidity* in its own votaries, and *persecution* towards other persons: And as temporal power alone can uphold such a system, it is generally a sure friend to *despotism*, with which on various accounts it makes a common cause.

This situation of this celebrated religion gives great encouragement for some sectary to arise, that steering a middle and successful course, shall strip it of its unnecessary and adventitious errors; and confine it chiefly to its creeds, its principal sacraments, its symbols, and its secular clergy.—A wise Catholic prince

prince would support such an advantageous attempt with his utmost influence; for, if really wise, he would see that despotism was not necessary to his happiness, scarcely so to his passions, and clearly not to his permanent grandeur, since it contaminates his subjects, who, in these times, are to be the only means of his grandeur. But, if the prince is really smitten with this ignoble vice, there are sovereigns who will teach him, that even a protestant may be despotic.

To assist the views of a wise prince, a scheme follows for annihilating the orders of monks and nuns in countries of the fiercest bigotry, with scarce a murmur, and which, from its efficacy and simplicity, may fit the grandest legislator.—*It is to distribute among the separate individuals of the religious houses, that wealth of which they have now only a joint use for life.* The prince who does this, must add to it the power of disposing of this share by testament, to relatives, friends, and pious persons specified by *name*; but not to any general, corporate, or entailed uses whatever.—Ought the prince to retain for himself any part? This is a local question, which, at the moment of the event, will probably be imprudently decided. Certainly, without retaining any thing, the prince will be *no loser* by the arrangement; certainly, his disinterestedness will acquire him confidence, success, and personal safety; and certainly princes of every description, will find that the wealth of their people will ultimately become their own.—There are other purposes, however, for which a prince ought to make a reserve. He ought to reserve something for those *designed to belong to these orders*, but the amount should be moderate, because the candidates will probably have youth on their side; and the wealth of the regular clergy, upon being put into circulation, will not return to the great people who gave it, but to those ranks chiefly that now enjoy it; and consequently younger children, and middling people, will have the same chances for provision as in other countries. The prince should make a second reserve for the *mendicant* regular clergy, because reforms are generally tranquil, when the whole body of those that are incumbents and interested are immediately satisfied. And, lastly, some temporary reserve should be made for the *poor*, who, by the sovereign's operations, will lose their daily gratuitous supplies; in addition to which assistance, they must immediately be provided with simple objects of employment, and foreigners be introduced (who, besides paying taxes, will in an age or two become natives) to teach the whole country that industry and ingenuity, of which probably it has hitherto had none or few examples. This done, the prince, in less than twenty years, may find his dominions in a state of considerable improvement.—Other schemes

schemes to get rid of this incubus, (the regular clergy) will probably be dreamt over for twenty years, and the country at last be found as far from relief as ever. May God then speed this *holy* work!

This preface will now conclude with a remark upon itself.—The book which it precedes will naturally be read before it, by the wit, the traveller, the picture-lover, the antiquarian, the ecclesiastic, and even the serious politician. But gaiety alone on these subjects might be thought deficient without argument, as argument would probably be inefficacious without gaiety; and, though both methods may not succeed at the same moment, and in the same instance, yet perhaps, on the whole, the one may not impede the influence of the other.—At all events, the writer of this preface had these objects in view: To prevent, as far as his influence can prevent, a tendency to persecution in these countries, upon reading the present stigma* on the popish orders of regular clergy; to spread ideas also that may be useful in promoting the reform or abolition of these orders in *old* catholic countries; and to warn against the introduction of these institutions in new countries, such as America and Ireland, where the catholic religion may soon meet with a new existence or indulgence.—Instead of these absurdities, valuable places of education should be established in each; which may prevent their papist citizens from going into foreign parts, to renew in themselves all the follies of their ancestors, and take up attachments to other countries, to the weakening of that which they ought to feel for ther own.

And let no Englishman be alarmed at this doctrine of innovation. Some of our bishops are at this instant said to be acting upon a similar plan †. They are recommending, as we are told, to the clergy in their dioceses, to prepare the people of England for an alteration in the form of the common prayer; being probably wisely persuaded that an established form does not mean a form that is *immutable*, but simply, that there shall always be *some* form established by law; that form to be regulated, as heretofore, by the heads of the Church, according to the lights of the times. [This appears to have been written in the year 1783.]

* That is, the stigma contained in Baron Born's book.
† The writer appears to have been under some considerable mistake here.

ARTICLE IV.

COPY *of a Letter from the Lord Bishop of* CLONFERT, *to the Rev. Mr.* MOORE, *of Boughton-Blean, near Canterbury.*

THOUGH I had not the pleasure of receiving your very informing discourse on Sunday schools at the time you intended, I having since got it, and read it with the greatest satisfaction. It is an admirable defence and recommendation of this new institution, which I hope will daily become more general, and produce the best moral effects, by impressing the children of the poor with a sense of duty and religion, at the only time and age when they are capable of impressions. A poor man's creed need not be long, but it should be struck in early, and a true and right one. If he believes, as the common proverb says, that he is to die like a dog, he will undoubtedly live like one.—The communication of education is certainly a very great blessing to the poor ; and had Mandeville, and they who, to serve political purposes, are for denying all instruction to the lower classes, only pushed their argument far enough, they might have proved, that they had a right to maim or put out the eyes of the common people, in order to make them more manageable, and more in the power of their superiors.

Having never seen the paragraph in the English papers concerning me, to which you allude in your appendix, I can say nothing to it; but what I have endeavoured to do in my diocese, ever since my appointment, is this:—There are twenty catholics to one protestant in it. To attempt their conversion, or to think of making them read protestant books, would be in vain ; I have therefore circulated amongst them some of the best of their own authors, particularly one Gother, whose writing contain much pure christianity, useful knowledge, and benevolent sentiments. He wrote eighteen volumes of religious extracts, and died about the year 1696. Unable to make the peasants about me good protestants, I wish to make them good catholics, good citizens, and good any thing. —I have established too a sunday school, open to both protestants and catholics, at my residence in the country ; have recommended the scheme to my clergy, and hope to have several on foot in the summer. Pastoral works, however, of this nature, go on very heavily in a kingdom so unsettled, and so intoxicated with politics as this is.; I return you my best thanks for your very obliging present.

ARTICLE V.

A Letter taken from the IRISH VOLUNTEERS JOURNAL, *March* 1786.

To Lord Viscount MOUNTGARRET.

My Lord,

THOUGH I live at a distance from the capital, and am no actor in public affairs, I am an attentive observer of what passes, and from a long habit of reading the public papers, I find that I can distinguish, with tolerable accuracy, the drift of most speakers.

I consider the *trade* of opposition (for I cannot call it by another name) as the most servile and illiberal which any gentleman can adopt; but a real independent man, who stands forth occasionally in the public service, and has the sagacity and firmness to choose solid and manly ground, appears to me in the light of an honorary minister; and as long as he is not paid by the king, he is entitled to a proportionable share of public consideration and confidence, as well as to the active support of every independent man without doors.

It is upon this account I presume to address your Lordship without the least personal knowledge of you, in consequence of what is said to have passed in the house of lords on Friday the 28th of January last. It gave me a particular satisfaction to find, while so many other members of both houses seemed to beat every bush to start some political game, that your lordship, with deep wisdom, laid your finger upon what I cannot help thinking with you, " the true cause of all those risings which, in such a course " of years, could not be brought to suppession." That it lies with the clergy to remove it, which must be done effectually before any solid foundation can be laid for our prosperity; and till it is done, every superstructure will prove frivolous and unstable.

I do not pretend to doubt the facts asserted by the right reverend and learned lords who spoke in answer to your lordship, nor do I conceive that it could be your meaning that *all* the disturbances which have at any time happened in the circuit of this large kingdom, were *immediately* occasioned by the severe and inconsiderate mode of collecting tithes, which yet very generally prevails; but neither do I conceive that your lordship, speaking as a legislator, could think yourself confined, as if you had been called on as a witness in a particular cause in a court of justice, to attest the immediate case of any individual's delinquency:

your

your lordship looked further, and meant doubtless to point out the real common cause of the general spirit of outrage, which is acknowledged on all hands to gain ground throughout this kingdom; and on that account you naturally were led to recur to the two fundamentals of all political society, *agriculture* and *morals*, as well as the particular grievance dwelt upon in that debate; and I own that I am astonished that your Lordship could, for a single moment, be considered upon such ground as an enemy to the clergy. I consider you, on the contrary, as their best friend, in forewarning the church of its unseen danger, and the clergy of an impending attack.

For my own part I dissemble not that I was bred up in abhorrence of popery, and I rejoice to see the day arrive which must convince the most bigotted and unobserving, of the fallacy and decay of that idolatrous mode of worship. Without appealing to the philosophical writings which abound through Europe, it suffices to observe the manner in which the order of St. Ignatius has been suppressed, by courts hitherto distinguished for their bigotry, and at length utterly extinguished by the pope, though in all times considered as the body guards of St. Peter's chair; and those same courts, it is well known, are proceeding to shake off every remains of papal tyranny, as fast as so great a change can well be supposed to take place, without an immediate mission from above.

Animated at once, and shamed by such examples from such quarters, I rejoice in the corresponding liberal spirit which daily more and more prevails throughout the British empire; and has induced the legislatures of Great Britain and Ireland to relax a mode, which as much dishonoured them both, as the height of superstition could do.

These are texts calculated to awaken and to impress the most unlettered and the most barbarous; but who is there to set them forth, and to do them justice? Is it our established ministry? I am attached to the church both by birth and inclination, and after what your lordship so truly stated, it hurts me, even generally, to allude to the non-residence of so many among the clergy—their numberless sinecures—pluralities unbounded—the general habits of luxury—and the spiritual lukewarmness even of the best, who content themselves with repeating, now and then, some cold essay; or once in their lives perhaps (God knows how rare the instances) publish some literary work, which has a little to do with the main duties of a parochial clergyman, such as we see it practised, even in the most catholic countries, as so much mathematics or natural philosophy would. Do those learned gentlemen suppose that the newspapers will quite supply their places, and inculcate lessons calculated to make their flocks happy here and hereafter?

But, put conscience and all sense of duty out of the question; let the matter be examined with a view to the simple question of *interest*. Does any reflecting clergyman, or any friend of the church suppose, that nearly two millions of catholics, open as they are to the practices of foreign powers, who know well enough how good a cloak religion still affords; how powerful an instrument it still remains—and two hundred and fifty thousand protestant dissenters, with the example of America, free before their eyes—they too—capable of enthusiasm, well instructed, and from every circumstance of character, situation, and connection, able both to concert and act, will long continue patiently to pay tythes to such immense amount, to idle, non-resident clergymen of the small number which remains?

Since the emancipation of this country, the minds of men have been occupied with the novelty of the revolution which has taken place. They naturally have been jealous of their title to so much unhoped for freedom; and their youthful eagerness has been directed to the bauble, as for some time it must be, of a free trade; but this has now nearly spent itself.

What then is there next more likely to strike the minds of an awakened, active people, whose national character is full of imagination and enterprize—who, fresh from so much political action and triumph, cannot all be expected to settle at Prosperous, and become half women under the direction of good Captain Brooke—What more, than the state of the clergy, and of the tythes at present collected? Is it not much better that they should occupy themselves so, than cabal with France, or Spain, or Austria; or than that the catholics and dissenters should set to cutting each others throats, which some cunning men, perhaps, might consider as the safest means of prolonging to the established clergy their present overflow of wealth?

What other string is there more promising to the touch of brilliant orators, brazen lawyers, and intriguing politicians; more likely to unite what is called the public, and to gain them that degree of confidence which they well know how to carry afterwards to market? In short, what other question so safe and sure?

Government is obliged of itself to come to Parliament for a new system of police: does it then require any great degree of foresight to be assured that the truth must soon bolt itself out, and the real sources of all the acknowledged outrages point out themselves, where there is nothing sufficient to impede them?

However uninlightened we may be thought, we have certainly got the length of knowing with your lordship, that *agriculture* and *morals* are the only true foundations of either free trade or police:—establish these better than any other country in Europe—your situation will make you masters of every thing else. Every blessing will naturally follow, independent of treaties or negociations, whether at home or abroad.

Ludlow,

Ludlow, somewhere in his memoirs relates, that Cromwell (alluding to Ireland) speaks of it as, in many particulars, clean paper; " where such laws might be enacted, and justice so im-" partially administered, *as to be a good precedent, even to England* " *itself.* Where, when they once observe property preserved and " improved at so easy and cheap a rate, they will never suffer " themselves to be so cheated and abused." Yet it was not Cromwell's object to *disunite* England and Ireland.

Now, will any rational, impartial friend of the church pretend that the clergy, in their present state advance the one, one-hundredth part as much as they impede the other? I earnestly wish that my lords, the bishops, and other wise men among the clergy, would reflect before it be too late: that they would survey for a moment the condition of the several works they have to defend—and then look at the nature, number, and circumstances of the army which they have to defend them.

I put all philosophy out of the question; but it might be expedient in them to look back a little, and think how all our present reformation is: under what a variety of disadvantages it took place: how imperfectly it extended itself to this country.—How barbarous the whole jurisdiction of the bishop's courts; how inconsonant with the common law of the land, and how much more so with the temper of our times? What the conviction of all Europe is, upon the subject of ecclesiastical rights; and what the proceedings which are now depending in different countries; but above all, where the citadel is to which they can retire in case of attack.—If the subject is once started, it will run like wildfire.

What body of men will stand out in their defence? Out of doors it is pretty plain, they have no manner of chance. Will the house of commons risque their tottering weight with the public in their behalf? I am afraid, that in this article they partake too much of the opinion of their constituents, for us to expect much partiality from them. If things once pass the house of commons, can the lords stop them, and my lords the bishops make a stand in their own persons, and in their own cause? I should be afraid of what happened to the Scotch bishops: and earnestly hope that their example would deter ours from so desperate a resolution. If the house of lords gave way to the temper of the times, I am afraid there is now no privy council within this kingdom able to stem the torrent; the only chance which would remain would be with the crown, and the privy council of England. And can any friend to the church suppose that the crown, after giving up Poyning's act, the point just alluded to regarding the privy council—the great point of legislative independency, and the English nation, after giving up her monopoly of our export and import trade, will draw their swords, and risque a general war in Europe (the probable consequence) on

account

account of a body of men, to whom they have so distant a relation? Besides, is the church popular enough in our sister kingdom? Or is administration there strong enough to force such a measure? Or is there any probability *of any* administration's taking place, which would be strong or willing enough to hazard such an undertaking! We should only deceive ourselves, if we suffered our minds to rely for a single moment on such a vain expectation.

Every man must be sensible, that I do not address your lordship with a view to inflame: so far from colouring or exaggerating any thing, I forbear to state even facts, or to enter into any detail whatever.

The archbishop of Cashel calls upon your lordship, *to lay your finger upon one single clergyman:* Does his grace then seriously defy your lordship to produce an instance of one profligate clergyman? I commend your lordship's reserve in that particular.—I augur well from it of your future conduct. If your lordship has descended to personality, I should never have thought of addressing you. I do not mean any more, than I hope your lordship does, to have recourse to strong facts or particular details, (though near at hand, and in every body's power) till things come to the last extremity: but to turn the eyes of the public another way, I read with pleasure, what his grace says in the same speech, " that " if your lordship would at any time bring forward any propositi- " ons, &c. that you should have every help in his power to car- " ry it into effect."

As a friend to the clergy, I only wish that his grace would go one step further, and that he, with the primate, and other good men in church and state, would themselves take the lead in this great matter, and by some timely sacrifices prevent inevitable danger. The sea is yet calm, the bishops and the government have as yet the helm in their own hands; but when the wind begins to blow, and a storm rises, who can tell the consequence? —Let some steps be taken this very session; there are some things so perfectly obvious, that I do not see the narrowest and most jealous churchman can fear their consequences; on the contrary, must readily discern the good effects which may be expected from them.

Let an end be immediately put to all dispensations; let every possibility of pluralities be for ever prevented; let residence be strictly enforced through the kingdom; let an act of parliament be passed to prevent any sinecures from being filled up, and to appropriate the revenues arising from each to a convenient house; and then, and not till then, let the clergy be nominated to them. It is to be hoped that churches will be built every where, in consequence of the encouragement already held out; if it is not sufficient, let it be increased: but supposing there be no church, it is no excuse for want of residence; a clergyman may

may and ought to do a great deal of good out of his church. Let every church preferment remain vacant for a compleat year after it falls, and the income be applied, in the first instance, to such improvements as may be indispensably necessary to enable residence; and afterwards, to the increase of small livings within the respective diocese, or within the kingdom at large, as may be judged most expedient. Let a commission be appointed, composed of bishops and judges, with the lord lieutenant to preside, in order to regulate the extent of all parishes; so that each parish may come within the immediate superintendance of one clergyman. Let a committee be appointed, of both houses of parliament, to consider of a general commutation throughout the kingdom for tythes *.

Other regulations may still suggest themselves: but if this much were done, I am satisfied it would avert the storm, and give the clergy a new, and, I hope, a perpetual lease of their situations; they would gain power, and would deserve it: instead of looking to government for support, they would be the support of it.

I earnestly hope that your lordship, as a friend to the church, will invite the spiritual lords in your house to stand forth in time, and take the honour and merit to themselves, of a new and timely reform, with the public. If they still seek to put off the evil day, it is to be hoped that your lordship will let the country know who among them are for, and who against a reform; and that some wise and moderate men will begin this necessary work, before those without doors shall think themselves obliged to take it in hand.

The history of Great Britain affords sufficient examples of the mischiefs which have resulted from delaying a redress of acknowledged grievances too long.

There was no wise man in the long parliament of the last century, who would not have wished to stop half way; but things were got into other hands, which did not know where to stop. That this may never be the case of the church of Ireland, is the sincere wish, but strong apprehension, of

A SON OF THE CLERGY.

* See what archdeacon Paley says upon the subject of tythes, in his book upon the principles of moral and political philosophy; a book lately published in England, admired and quoted by different descriptions of men. Speaking of tythes, he says, " The burthen of the tax falls with its chief, if not its " whole weight, upon tillage; that is to say, upon that precise mode of cul-
" tivation which, as has been shewn above, it is the business of the state to
" relieve and remunerate in preference to every other. No measure of such
" extensive concern appears to me so practicable, nor any single alteration so
" beneficial, as the conversion of tythes into corn-rents. This commutation
" I am convinced might be so adjusted, as to secure to the tythe-holder a com-
" pleat and perpetual equivalent for his interest, and to leave to industry its
" full operation, and entire reward." If this is the case in England, how much stronger does the necessity apply to Ireland; and how much more is the interest of the clergy of Ireland to accommodate for the reasons I have stated?

ARTICLE

ARTICLE VI.

Arguments selected from Bishop Hoadley's Refutation of Bishop Sherlock's Arguments concerning the Test and Corporation Acts.

1. Dr. Sherlock says, 'that the Protestant Church of England has 'enjoyed but little peace from its first establishment P;' and he attributes this want of peace, in part, to those who fled from England in the reign of queen Mary, 'and brought back those notions which 'have given this church and nation so much trouble ever since.— 'These,' he says, 'were one great occasion of the disturbance in 'Queen Elizabeth's reign.—Under the *management* of James I. the 'disaffection to the established church grew strong; and in the days 'of his unfortunate son, a prince who deserved a better fate, it pre- 'vailed as well against the crown as the mitre.'

These observations are intended by the Dean to shew the necessity of such acts as the Test and Corporation Acts, in order to exclude all who dissent from the established church from offices of power and trust in the nation.—Now, let any man set himself down to the reading of the rise, progress, and issue of all this unhappy part of our history, and let him weigh all circumstances impartially within his own breast; and then let him judge whether this very history, from the days of queen Elizabeth, will not itself furnish a strong argument for the very contrary to what the Dean is going to infer from it. For, if he finds that it is an history of the effects of the passions of men, set on fire by hardships and exclusions, made outrageous merely for want of an universal mutual forbearance, carried to their height by oppressions and difficulties for the sake of differences in religion, he will judge between the *Dean*'s argument drawn from hence, and what *I* would infer.—*His* argument is this: 'There has been long a disaffection to 'the church; and this disaffection has heretofore broke out into 'violences, and at last prevailed against both the crown and the 'mitre. Therefore, it is just and wise now to exclude all from civil 'offices who dissent from the church.'—*My* argument is this: 'All 'this disaffection was continually heightened by the hardships and 'pressures put upon those who at all disapproved of any thing in the 'established church, even though constant conformists to it. Their 'suffering in their civil rights upon religious accounts, was the 'inflaming consideration, and what gave fire to their passions, which 'at last produced such effects. The contrary, therefore, would have 'the contrary effect. Let all hardships, and all oppressions, little and 'great, cease: let there be no civil punishment, or civil suffering,

'or

'or civil inconvenience (call it, as the Dean pleafes,) on the account
'of what is the dictate of men's private confciences, unlefs it imme-
'diately affect the civil government; and I cannot but think there
'would be an end of the keennefs of the difaffection itfelf, and of all
'the paffionate effects of it.' At leaft, there is this probability for it:
the former method has been tried, and has been fo far from diminifhing
it, that it has been feen to blow it up into violence and force; and even
to excufe this violence by the fame pretence of felf-defence againft
thofe who had practifed feverities againft their fellow fubjects upon
that fame foundation. The latter has never yet been tried wholly and
effectually. The degree in which it has been tried has been feen to
have mollified, and not fharpened that difaffection throughout the
nation: and the greater the degree is, the greater in proportion will
the effect be.

2. When Dr. Sherlock ftates the abolition of monarchy and epifcopa-
cy, during the civil war, and reafons upon it, his argument amounts to
this:—That in *King Charles's days*, thofe who then diffented from the
Church of England, having got power and opportunitiy, prevailed
againft the crown; overturned the civil conftitution; eftablifhed their
own church; and as much as in them lay, abolifhed the government,
difcipline, and worfhip of the church which was, before this, the
eftablifhed church the ecclefiaftical conftitution of the realm; which
is always fuppofed to be part of the government. *Therefore*, it was juft
and wife, after the Reftoration, to exclude all by law, from places of
power and truft, who differed at that time from the eftablifhed Church
of England. And, therefore, likewife (which I beg of the reader
particularly to obferve, as it is the whole defign of the Dean's book,
though very much neglected and very little laboured by him,) it is juft
and right *ftill to continue* to exclude all Nonconformifts at prefent,
about fixty years [r] after that time, from all capacity of holding offices:
to which capacity they have an undoubted right, were it not for fuch
a law of exclufion; or were it not for their nonconformity. The
remonftrances againft the crown and the mitre both, and the civil war
itfelf, were begun and carried on by *churchmen*; by conftant churchmen; by a parliament full of churchmen. This was the grand original
and occafion of thofe evils which come afterwards; though unex-
pected and undefigned by thofe who firft began.—But what I argue
is this: that, if it be good reafoning to infer from paft proceedings
that the followers of fuch and fuch perfons, in fome of their main
principles, may juftly be excluded from offices of power and truft; it
will follow from hence, that it had been juft in King Charles II. and

---

[r] Upwards of fixty years more muft now be added to the calculation, as that time
is elapfed fince the publication of Bifhop Hoadly's book; or confiderably more than
a century in the whole.

his

his administration, to have excluded from offices of power and trust, all persons who would not solemnly renounce and detest those first proceedings in defence of liberty and property, and the principles of those first patriots who actually began a war with the crown, which was the inlet to all the calamities and evils which the Dean mentions.

To exclude Nonconformists from all offices of power and trust now, because some who did not like the Church of England, in former days, were guilty of great iniquity, and abolished the establishment of that church when they had power in their hands; is a remedy, of no relation to the disease; because all those evils were not the effects of any such former law, by which Nonconformists were capable of offices: and, therefore, the making any such exclusive law, since that time, cannot be justified by those evils. The power which any Nonconformists then arrived at, was not the effect of any law in being, or the consequence of their being capable of holding offices under King Charles I.-- But the state of that matter was thus; that multitudes of the churchmen themselves were alarmed not only at the crown but at the mitre. They had great jealousies and suspicions of evil designs: they demanded a redress of many grievances: and, at length made open war with the crown. The nature of human affairs is always such, in all quarrels of so public a nature, that evils follow thick upon one another. This rupture increasing and growing wider by degrees, made way for any, who could, to seize the power: and they have the civil power, in such cases, who can get and maintain the strongest and most successful army. Now this being the state of the case, that not so much as the beginning or the least degree of these evils proceeded from any legal capacity of Nonconformists for offices under King Charles I. but rather from the hardships put upon these, as well as upon many churchmen themselves, in their religious rights as well as civil; it cannot possibly be made an argument, that Nonconformists ought now to be excluded from all offices of power and trust.

The Dean constantly hides from his readers what the justice of an historian (for such he here is) cannot deny even to those whom he exceedingly dislikes and disapproves, viz. that King Charles II. was actually *restored* to his kingdom by the help at least of one great party of Dissenters from our church. Several ministers of one persuasion waited on him, with whom he declared himself entirely satisfied as to their peaceable dispositions. The army, without which he could not have been restored, was of the same persuasion. It was, well known and thoroughly perceived, that episcopacy and the public worship of the Church of England, were of necessity to be (as to the main branches of them) restored with him. Nor was any reluctance to this in general expressed; but a great deal of joy and satisfaction in the whole affair.—This, I say, should have been remembered, by one

one who professes to enter with so much reluctance upon the bad side of those affairs: and it should have been remembered as some small amends, at least, some mark of dislike of what had passed, some token of no disaffection to the King or his government.—These particulars were so remarkable whilst the impression was fresh, that the Lord Chancellor Clarendon, in a speech to the parliament, Sept. 13, 1660, in the King's presence, described the army then to be disbanded to be little less than invincible, and 'an army whose order and discipline, 'whose sobriety and manners, whose courage and success had made it 'famous and terrible over the world,' in order to shew the King's sense of his obligation to it. And as to others also, the same noble Lord, at the meeting of the following parliament, in his speech to the House of Lords, called upon them to 'consider how much they owed 'to those who, with all the faculties of their souls, contributed to 'and contrived the blessed change; and then how much they owed to 'those who gave no opposition to the virtuous activity of others; and 'God knows (says he) a little opposition might have done much 'harm, &c.'—In this strain were matters spoken of (till new views produced new language), even openly and by authority. And therefore the Dean, amidst all his historical notices, need not have been ashamed or afraid to have done justice, common justice, to those upon whom he was now going to put hardship enough, and to bind it upon them with all the strength of that noble topic of self-defence.

When all this, together with the promises solemnly made at that time, shall be considered, every one will see that, if something else besides self-preservation had not been meant, such acts could not so soon have been thought of. Nor was it long in that reign, before the most serious churchmen as well as others, saw very plainly that the disuniting of Protestants from one another and the strengthening the contrary interest, and the bringing in new measures (or rather the madness) of loyalty, by extravagant addresses from the corporations of England, were ends more certainly in the view of some at that time, than the preservation of the gentlemen of the Church of England (as the Dean puts it), who were then in no danger, as I know of, but from themselves. This account of the fact, from whatever root these proceedings sprung, should not have been omitted—and then an argument of another sort would have offered itself, to this effect: Since it is certain that one sort of Nonconformists bore a great part in restoring the King, and multitude of Dissenters expressed an entire acquiescence in it; and since the King himself openly professed great satisfaction in them, and made promises not to forget this: it follows from hence, either that the evil spirits mentioned in the preamble of the Corporation Act were not the Nonconformists, as such, or else that this preamble (as it is with many others) does not give us the true reasons of the bill, and therefore cannot be alleged as any certain proof of the necessity of it; though it is urged for this purpose by Dr. Sherlock.

3. As the Dean's whole argument is founded upon this particular Church being the ecclesiastical constitution of the realm; upon the force of those principles which belong to civil governments and communities; upon declarations of acts of parliament; and upon the remembrance of past transactions; it will be evident, that all the like proceedings are just, wise, fitting, reasonable, and necessary in Scotland *against* the Church of England; which are declared by him to be fitting, wise, reasonable, and necessary in England for the *sake* of the Church of England. For the two kingdoms being now effectually united, it unluckily happens, that we have two ecclesiastical constitutions of the same realm. Both of these are equally, in the same strong words, declared by the laws of men in this realm, to be essential and fundamental to that union; the one in the south, the other in the north. In the south, the members of the Kirk of Scotland, as well as all who differ from our Church, are Dissenters. In the north, the members of the Church of England, and all who differ from that Kirk.

The whole of Dr. Sherlock's book is, indeed, of an admirable and almost unequalled comprehension. It sheds its kind influences upon all churches equally; by making it wise and just, for every one of them to be defended against the others, by oppression upon the members of others. It is particularly of two differing complexions, and has two different tendencies, in this same realm, in which we happen to have two very differing ecclesiastical constitutions.—As it is printed at London, it is a defence of the Church of England, as by law established, against all Nonconformists; by shewing the reasonableness of excluding them from all offices of power and trust. Let it be printed at Edinburgh, with the change of a few names and words; and the history of the destruction of the Kirk put instead of that of the destruction of the Church of England; and I will answer for it, it is, with equal justice and truth, a defence of the Kirk of Scotland, as by law established; shewing the justice, reasonableness, and necessity of excluding from all offices and posts of any power and trust all Nonconformists, and particularly all episcopal men; all who do not enter into the scheme of the confession of faith there established; all who are fond of any other scheme, as of the religion delivered by Christ. The argument will be the same there as it is here.

That way of reasoning which by necessary consequence leads to open and cruel persecution of Dissenters in all countries, which justifies the inquisition itself against all Protestants, which justifies the greatest violences of the late King of France against the Protestants there; which not only permits all this, but directs and guides Christians to mutual oppressions, and mutual injuries, without number and without end; and which will ever continue to do so: Such a way of reasoning, I say, cannot be just.—But the Dean's way of reasoning is of this sort: and, therefore, cannot be just in the

account

account of any Chriſtian or Proteſtant, who will but carefully examine into its foundation, and trace out the natural and unavoidable conſequences of it.

4. Dr. Sherlock endeavours to prove, that it is as juſtifiable for the government or the magiſtrate, to require the ſacramental teſt, as it is to require the ſecurity of an *oath*. 'When the magiſtrate (ſays he) ' requires an oath, he lays hold on the natural ſenſe and obligation ' we are under to believe in, and to fear God; and grounds the teſt ' on them. When he requires the ſacramental teſt, he lays hold of ' the obligation we are under to communicate with that Church, ' which we eſteem to be a true part of the Church of Chriſt; and ' grounds the teſt on it.

This is manifeſtly a very partial and a very miſtaken parallel, as to any juſtification it affords the magiſtrates, in the caſe before us. And I will beg leave to put it as follows:

When the magiſtrate requires an oath for the purpoſes of civil intereſt, or in order to poſſeſs a civil office, he requires a thing which was never appointed by God, or by Chriſt, to any other purpoſe; a thing which is in its own nature peculiarly fitted for purpoſes of this world upon this very account, becauſe it ſuppoſes, in the generality of men, a fear of ſome Superior Being, the avenger of falſehood and injuſtice; a thing which is the only proper inſtrument of what it is applied to, and in the application of which no partiality, in any degree, is implied or deſigned; and a thing which, though it may be abuſed by the wickedneſs of men, yet is the neceſſary, and perhaps the only means of the end propoſed: which renders the law requiring it, juſt and not chargeable with thoſe abuſes.

Now, in the other caſe, when the magiſtrate (that is, the lawmaker) requires the ſacramental teſt, in order to the poſſeſſion of civil offices, he requires an action to be done for this worldly purpoſe, which our Lord himſelf has appropriated to *another* and a ſpiritual purpoſe; and by ſuch appointment has in effect conſecrated and dedicated to one ſole uſe of quite another nature, and to quite another end; an action which has nothing in its inſtitution, nothing in its nature, that bears any relation to the purpoſes of civil life, and therefore is not a proper inſtrument of what it is applied to: an action to be performed after ſuch a peculiar manner, as implies in it a diſtinction to be put by it between ſome civil ſubjects and others equally good civil ſubjects, and makes that an inſtrument of partiality and animoſity, which was ordained by Chriſt as an inſtrument of the ſtricteſt union and affection between all his followers: an action, made neceſſary to the promotion of Infidels, who have no part in it, and yet muſt perform it, for that end: an action which they, who ordain and continue it for this purpoſe, know muſt lead to thoſe abuſes which the Dean ſays he ſees and laments: an action, neither the only nor the

the proper security against any evils, and, consequently, not necessary for that purpose: which consideration makes it impossible to justify a law, which unnecessarily enacts what naturally and unavoidably leads to such evils.

And now, let any one judge of the exact parallel between the sacramental test, which is the use of the holy sacrament for purposes very different from what it was ordained for; and the use of oaths, which is the use of what are fit and proper for the purposes they are appointed for. And if these considerations are not enough to satisfy Christians, I confess, I shall despair of their being made sensible of any thing.

ARTICLE VII.

Testimonies taken from the Appendix to the new Edition of Bishop Hoadly's Reply to Bishop Sherlock.

' EXcepting three sermons, preached on public occasions, Dr. Sher-
' lock's first appearance as an author, was in the famous Bangorian
' Controversy; and he was, by far, the most powerful antagonist
' Bishop Hoadly had. He published a great number of pamphlets upon
' this occasion; the principal of which is intituled, " A vindication of
" the Corporation and Test acts, in answer to the Bishop of Bangor's
" reasons for the repeal of them 1718." To this Bishop Hoadly
' replied; yet, while he opposed strenuously the principles of his ad-
' versary, he gave the strongest testimony to his abilities, calling his
' book, " the most plausible and ingenious defence that he thinks had
" ever been published, of excluding men from their acknowledged civil
" rights on account of differences in religion, or in the circumstances
" of religion."—It has been said, *Bishop Sherlock afterwards dis-*
' *approved the part he took in this dispute, and would never suffer his*
' *pamphlets to be re-printed.*'—See Dr. Sherlock's Life prefixed to his Discourses, 6th Edit. 1772.

TO the preceding Treatise of Bishop HOADLY's, it may not be improper here to subjoin the testimonies of two other eminent and learned Divines of the Church of England, in support of the propriety of a Repeal of the Test and Corporation Acts.

Dr. ARTHUR ASHLEY SYKES, a clergyman of distinguished abilities and worth, published, in 1736, a piece, entitled, ' The Reasonableness ' of applying for the Repeal or Explanation of the Corporation and Test ' Acts impartially considered f.' In this tract Dr. Sykes says, ' The

---
f See the Rev. Dr. DISNEY's accurate and valuable life of Dr. SYKES, published in 1785.

' Protestant

'Proteſtant Diſſenters are known to be as hearty, and as ſincere ſubjects
' to the King as any other ſubjects in his Majeſty's dominions g;'
and he therefore contends, that no other teſt ought to be required of
them, on their being admitted to places of truſt and power, but the
oaths of allegiance and ſupremacy, and the declaration againſt Popery.

The ſame year Dr. Sykes alſo publiſhed a pamphlet, entitled, 'The
' Corporation and Teſt Acts ſhewn to be of no Importance to the
' Church of England.' In this piece Dr. Sykes ſays, ' The govern-
' ment of the Church by biſhops is the ſame, and ſo it was long before
' the Teſt Act was made. The repeal of it does not deſtroy their
' ſeats in parliament, nor take away their baronies, nor deprive them of
' their juriſdiction; nor any ways affect them in their powers, or pro-
' perties, or perſons. They are left exactly in the ſame ſtate as they were
' both before this act was paſſed, and which they have been in ever ſince
' this act has exiſted. The inferior clergy are exactly the ſame; no
' ways touched in their perſons, privileges, or properties. The church
' laity are the ſame, excepting that they will not be obliged to
' turn the ſacrament of the Lord's Supper into any political tool,
' or make it an inſtrument applicable to uſes, for which our Lord
' and Saviour never intended it. Diſſenters, indeed, will be helped;
' an *incapacity* to them will be removed: but is this a change of *con-*
' *ſtitution* in either church or ſtate, more than the repeal of any preſent
' act of parliament makes, which gives an eaſe or help to any particular
' perſons whatever? The conſtitution of the church is the ſame
' now, that is was before the Teſt Act paſſed; and ſo it would be ſtill
' were the Teſt repealed, unleſs it be ſaid to be altered by every act of
' parliament that paſſes in relation to the church. And if this may
' be admitted, then the conſtitution of the church has been altered
' threeſcore times within theſe threeſcore years; and ſtill the church
' ſubſiſts, and flouriſhes, and has received no damage by ſuch changes.
At the cloſe of this piece, he ſays, ' And now I leave the reader to
' judge, whether the ſacramental teſt be of any importance either to
' church or ſtate; whether it be not a real prejudice to Chriſtianity it-
' ſelf; and whether that which is prejudicial to Chriſtianity can be of
' importance to the Church of England.—Or if one conſiders the ſtate
' diſtinct from the church, it is an injury to take away men's rights,
' which they have never forfeited; it is weakening the ſtate itſelf, it is a
' hardſhip put upon the government, and no one ſingle good can poſ-
' ſibly be obtained to the ſtate by it. The continuance, therefore, of

---

g The Reaſonableneſs of applying for the Repeal, &c. p. 19.
i The Corporation and Teſt Acts ſhewn to be of no importance to the
Church of England, p. 34, 35.

' ſuch

' such a test has much evil, and no good. It is a real damage to
' Christianity, and a grief to all its most serious professors k.'

The reverend and learned Mr. PALEY, Archdeacon of Carlisle, in his " Principles of Moral and Political Philosophy," makes the following observations: ' Toleration is of two kinds: the allowing
' to Dissenters the unmolested profession and exercise of their re-
' ligion, but with an exclusion from offices of trust and emolument
' in the state, which is a *partial* toleration; and the admitting them,
' without distinction, to all the civil privileges and capacities of other
' citizens, which is a *complete* toleration.—The expediency of tole-
' ration, and consequently the right of every citizen to demand it,
' as far as relates to liberty of conscience, and the claim of being
' protected in the free and safe profession of his religion, is deducible
' from the second of those propositions, which we have delivered as the
' grounds of our conclusions upon the subject. That proposition
' asserts truth, and truth in the abstract, to be the supreme perfection of
' every religion. The advancement, consequently, and discovery of
' truth, is that end to which all regulations concerning religion
' ought principally to be adapted. Now, every species of intolerance
' which enjoins suppression and silence, and every species of persecution
' which enforces such injunctions, is adverse to the progress of truth;
' forasmuch as it causes that to be fixed by one set of men, at one time,
' which is much better and with much more probability of success, left
' to the independant and progressive enquiries of separate individuals,
' Truth results from discussion and from controversy: is investigated
' by the labours and researches of private persons. Whatever therefore
' prohibits these, obstructs that industry and that liberty which
' it is the common interest of mankind to promote l.'—The confining
' of the subject to the religion of the state, is a needless violation
' of natural liberty, and in an instance in which constraint is always
' grievous. Persecution produces no sincere conviction, nor any real
' change of opinion. On the contrary, it vitiates the public morals
' by driving men to prevarication, and commonly ends in a general,
' though secret, infidelity, by imposing under the name of revealed
' religion, systems of doctrine which men cannot believe and dare
' not examine m.' When we examine the sects of Christianity,
' which actually prevail, in the world, we must confess, that with
' the single exception of refusing to bear arms, we find no tenet in
' any of them, which incapacitates men for the service of the state.
' It has, indeed, been asserted, that discordancy of religions, even

---

k The Corporation and Test Acts shewn to be of no Importance to the Church of England, p. 71, 72.
l Principles of Moral and Political Philosophy, p. 578, 579. Second edit:
m Principles of Moral and Political Philosophy, p. 580.

supposing

'supposing each religion to be free from any errors that affect the safety or the conduct of government, is enough to render men unfit to act together in public stations. But upon what argument, or upon what experience, is this assertion founded? I perceive no reason why men of different religious persuasions may not sit upon the same bench, deliberate in the same council, or fight in the same ranks, as well as men of various or opposite opinions upon any controverted topic of natural philosophy, history, or ethics [n].'

In 1769 and 1772, the ministers among the Dissenters applied to Parliament for relief from the obligation they were then under to subscribe the doctrinal articles of the Church of England in order to be entitled to a toleration, and both times succeeded in the House of Commons, in consequence of LORD NORTH's neutrality, but were defeated in the House of Lords, in consequence of an opposition from the Episcopal Bench. They persevered, however; the Bishops repented; and a third application proved successful in both Houses.—In the debate occasioned in the House of Lords by the *second* application, Dr. Drummond, the Archbishop of York, having called the Dissenting Ministers " men of close ambition," Lord CHATHAM said, that this was judging uncharitably; and that whoever brought such a charge against them, without proof, defamed. Here he paused; and then went on—" The Dissenting Ministers are represented as men of close ambition. They are so, my Lords; and their ambition is to keep *close* to the college of fishermen, not of cardinals, and to the doctrine of inspired apostles, not to the decree of interested and aspiring bishops. They contend for a spiritual creed, and scriptural worship: We have a Calvinistic creed, a Popish liturgy, and an Armenian clergy. The Reformation has laid open the scriptures to all: Let not the Bishops shut them again. Laws in support of ecclesiastical power are pleaded for which it would shock humanity to execute. It is said, that religious sects have done great mischief, when they were not kept

---

[n] Ibid, p. 582.——The same author, reasoning from premises like Bishop Warburton's, nevertheless ends with the following declaration.—' A comprehensive national religion, guarded by a few articles of peace and conformity, together with a legal permission for the clergy of that religion, and a *complete* toleration of all dissenters from the established church, without any other limitation or exception, than what arises from the conjunction of dangerous political dispositions with certain religious tenets; appears to be not only the most just and liberal, but *the wisest and safest system* which a state can adopt; inasmuch as it unites the several perfections which a religious constitution ought to aim at;—liberty of conscience, with means of instruction; the progress of truth, with the peace of society; the right of private judgment, with the care of the public safety.'

" under

" under restraint: but history affords no proof that sects have ever
" been mischievous, when they were not oppressed and persecuted
" by the ruling church." See the Parliamentary Debates for 1772.

In one of his letters to a friend, not long after this debate, dated Burton-Pynsent, January 16, 1773, he expresses himself in the following words: " In writing to you, it is impossible the mind should
" not go of itself to that most interesting of all objects to fallible
" man—TOLERATION. Be assured, that on this sacred and un-
" alienable right of nature, and bulwark of truth, my warm wishes
" will always keep pace with your own. Happy, if the times had
" allowed us to add hopes to our wishes."

ARTICLE VIII.

Extracts from Mr. Locke's first letter concerning Toleration.

THE commonwealth seems to me to be a society of men, constituted only for the procuring, preserving, and advancing their own civil interests. Civil interests, I shall call life, liberty, health, and indolency of body; and the possession of outward things, such as money, lands, houses, furniture, and the like. It is the duty of the civil magistrate, by the impartial execution of equal laws, to secure unto all the people in general, and to every one of his subjects in particular, the just possession of these things belonging to this life. If any presume to violate the laws of public justice and equity established for the preservation of those things, his presumption is to be checked by the fear of punishment, consisting of the deprivation or diminution of those civil interests or goods which otherwise he might and ought to enjoy. But seeing no man does willingly suffer himself to be punished by the deprivation of any part of his goods, and much less his liberty or life, therefore is the magistrate armed with the force and strength of all his subjects, in order to the punishment of all those that violate any other man's right.

Now that the whole jurisdiction of the magistrate reaches only to these civil concernments; and that all civil power, right, and dominion, is founded and confined to the only care of promoting these things; and that it neither can, nor ought in any manner, to be extended to the salvation of souls, these following considerations seem unto me abundantly to demonstrate.

First, because the care of souls is not committed to the civil magistrate any more than to other men. It is not committed unto
him

him, I say, by God; because it appears not that God has ever given any such authority to one man over another, as to compel any one to his religion. Nor can any such power be vested in the magistrate, by the consent of the people; because no man can so far abandon the care of his own salvation, as blindly to leave it to the choice of any other whether prince or subject, to prescribe to him what faith or worship he shall embrace: for no man can, if he would, conform his faith to the dictates of another. All the life and power of true religion consist in the inward and full persuasion of the mind; and faith is not faith without believing. Whatever profession we make, to whatever outward worship we conform, if we are not fully satisfied in our own mind that the one is true, and the other well pleasing to God, such profession and such practice far from being any furtherance, are indeed great obstacles to our salvation. For in this manner instead of expiating our sins by the exercise of religion, I say, in offering thus unto God Almighty such a worship as we esteem to be displeasing unto him, we add unto the number of our other sins, those also of hypocrisy and contempt of his divine majesty.

In the second place. The care of souls cannot belong to the civil magistrate, because his power consists only in outward force; but true and saving religion consists in the inward persuasion of the mind, without which nothing can be acceptable to God. It may indeed be alledged that the magistrate may make use of arguments, and thereby draw the heterodox into the way of truth, and procure their salvation.—I grant it; but this is common to him with other men. In teaching, instructing, and redressing the erroneous by reason, he may certainly do what becomes *any* good man to do. Magistracy does not oblige him to put off either humanity or christianity. But it is one thing to persuade, and another thing to command; one thing to press with arguments, another with penalties. This the civil power alone has a right to do; to the other, goodwill is authority enough. Every man has a commission to admonish, exhort, and convince another of error, and by reasoning to draw him into truth: but to give laws, receive obedience, and compel with the sword, belongs to none but the magistrate.— And upon this ground I affirm, that the magistrate's power extends not to the establishing of any articles of faith, or forms of worship, by the force of his laws: for laws are of no force at all without penalties, and penalties in this case are absolutely impertinent, because they are not proper to convince the mind. Neither the profession of any articles of faith nor the conformity to any outward form of worship (as has been already said) can be available to the salvation of souls, unless the truth of the one, and the acceptableness of the other unto God be thoroughly believed by those who so profess

profess and practice: but penalties are no ways capable to produce such a belief.—It is only light and evidence, that can work a change in men's opinions, which light can in no manner proceed from corporal sufferings or any other outward penalties.

In the third place. The care of the salvation of men's souls cannot belong to the magistrate; because though the rigour of the laws and the force of penalties were capable to convince and change men's minds, yet would not that help at all to the salvation of their souls. For there being supposed to be but one truth, one way to heaven; what hope is there that more men would be led into it, if they had no rule but the religion of the court, and were put under a necessity to quit the light of their own reason and oppose the dictates of their own consciences, and blindly to resign up themselves to the will of their governors, and to the religion which either ignorance, ambition or superstition had chanced to establish in the countries where they were born?—In the variety and contradiction of opinions in religion (wherein the princes of the world are as much divided, as in their secular interests) the "narrow way" would be much straitened; one country alone would be in the right; and all the rest of the world put under an obligation of following their princes, in the ways that lead to destruction; and that, which heightens the absurdity and very ill suits the notion of a deity, men would owe their eternal happiness or misery to the places of their nativity.

These considerations, to omit many others that might have been urged to the same purpose, seem unto me sufficient to conclude, that all the power of civil government relates only to men's civil interests; is confined to the care of the things of this world; and has nothing to do with the world to come.

But after all, the principal consideration, and which absolutely determines this controversy is this. Although the magistrates' opinion in religion be sound, and the way that he appoints be truly evangelical; yet if I be not thoroughly persuaded thereof, in my own mind, there will be no safety for me, in following it. No way whatsoever that I shall walk in, against the dictates of my conscience, will ever bring me to the mansions of the blessed. I may grow rich by an art that I take no delight in; I may be cured of some disease by remedies that I have no faith in; but I cannot be saved by a religion that I distrust, and a worship that I abhor. It is in vain for an unbeliever to take up the outward shew of another man's profession; faith only and inward sincerity, are the things that procure acceptance with God. The most likely and most approved remedy can have no effect upon the patient, if his stomach reject it as soon as taken. And you will in vain cram a medicine down a sick man's throat, which his particular constitution will be sure

sure to turn into poison.—In a word; whatsoever may be doubtful in religion, yet this is at least certain, that no religion, which I believe not to be true, can be either true or profitable unto me. In vain therefore do princes compel their subjects to come into their church communion, under pretence of saving their souls. If they believe, they will come of their own accord: if they believe not, their coming will nothing avail them.—How great soever, in fine, may be the pretence of good will and charity, and concern for the salvation of men's souls, men cannot be forced to be saved whether they will or no. And therefore, when all is done, they must be left to their *own* consciences.

ARTICLE IX.

Extracts from the Essays on POPULATION, *printed in " the " Repository, containing various political, philosophical, literary " and miscellaneous articles, for* 1788."

'IN my opinion,' says Sir Josiah Child, as quoted by this writer, 'contending for *uniformity in religion* has contributed ten
' times more to the depopulation of Spain, than all the American
' plantations. What was it but *that*, which caused the expulsion
' of so many thousand Moors, who had built and inhabited most of
' the chief towns in Andalusia, and other parts? What was it but
' *that*, and the inquisition, that has and does expel such vast num-
' bers of rich Jews, with their families and estates, into Germany,
' Italy, Turkey, Holland and England? What was it but *that*,
' which caused those vast and long wars between that king and the
' Low Countries, and the effusion of so much blood and treasure,
' and the loss of the Seven Provinces, which we now see so pro-
' digiously rich and full of people, while *Spain* is empty and poor,
' and Flanders thin and weak, in continual fear of being made a
' prey to their neighbours.—Holland now sends as many, and
' more people, yearly, to reside in their plantations, fortresses,
' and ships in the East-Indies (besides many into the Indies).
' than Spain, and yet are so far from declining in the number of
' their people at home, that it is evident they do monstrously
' increase; and so I hope to prove, that England has constantly
' increased in people at *home*, since our settlement upon plantations
' in America.'

In another place the author of the above essays writes as follows. Much might be said on the subject of the mode of planting colonies, of their proper feats, their proper objects, and the proper systems for their government; but this would not only open a wide field, but would produce divided opinions. I shall therefore conclude with the notice only of two circumstances respecting colonies.

The first regards *morals*. The late Mr. Richard Jackson excellently remarks on this subject, as follows: ' When we would form
' a people, soil and climate may be found at least sufficiently good;
' inhabitants may be encouraged to settle, and even supported for a
' while; a good government and laws may be framed, and even arts
' may be established, or their produce imported. But many necessary
' moral habits are hardly ever found among those, who voluntarily
' offer themselves in times of *quiet* at home, to people new colonies;
' besides that, the moral as well as mechanical habits, adapted to
' the mother country, are frequently not so to the new-settled one,
' and to external events, many of which are always unforeseen.
' Hence it is we have seen such fruitless attempts to settle colinies,
' at an immense public and private expence, by several of the powers
' of Europe; and it is particularly observable, that none of the
' *English* colonies became any way considerable, till the necessary
' manners were born and grew up in the country, excepting those
' to which singular circumstances at home forced manners fit for
' the forming of a new state *.'—We may add to this passage, that good morals have a tendency to suppress the vices which waste the human race, and at the same time to introduce grave and important pursuits. They offer, under the restraint of marriage, a system which is the most productive possible respecting the *birth* of children; and which, by giving to each parent confidence in the fidelity of the other, unites them both in the care of rearing their offspring, and inclines them both to form a settled home, and to establish a fund of permanent property.—Dr. Davenant had a very imperfect idea of our general theory, but he very well elucidates this part of it, in speaking of the particular instance of English North America.
' To the sobriety and temperate manner of living, practised by the
' *dissenters* in America,' he says,' ' we may justly attribute the in-
' crease they have made there of inhabitants, which is beyond the
' usual proportion to be any where else observed. The supplies
' from Europe by no means answer their present numbers; it must
' therefore follow, that their thrift, and regular manner of living,
' incline them more to marry, and make them more healthful for
' generation, and afford them better means of having the necessaries
' to sustain life, as wholesome food and cleanly dwelling and apparel;
' the want of which, in other countries, is a high article in the
' burials of the common people. We do not pretend here to excuse

* See R. J's remarks on Dr. Franklin's Thoughts on the Peopling of Countries, &c. printed with Dr. Franklin's works.

' the

' the heterodox opinions these dissenters from our church may have
' conceived about religious matters, nor to justify their schism;
' but it must be owned, that the sobriety, which at least they pos-
' sess outwardly, is beneficial, both in practice and example: For
' where riot and luxuries are not discountenanced, the inferior rank
' of men become presently infected, and grow lazy, effeminate,
' impatient of labour, and expensive, and consequently cannot
' thrive by trade and tillage. So that when we contemplate the
' great increase and improvement, which have been made in New
' England, Carolina, and Pennsylvania, we cannot but think it
' injustice not to say, that a large share of this general good to
' those parts, is owing to the education of their planters; which,
' if not entirely virtuous, has a shadow of virtue; and if this only
' were an appearance, it is yet better for a people that are to sub-
' sist in a new country by traffic and industry, than the open pro-
' fession of lewdness, which is always attended with national decay
' and poverty.'—To this same effect we find Sir Josiah Child and
archbishop Sharp speaking. Sir Josiah says, with respect to New
England. ' I am now to write of a people, whose frugality, in-
' dustry and temperance, and the happiness of whose laws and in-
' stitutions, promise to them a wonderful increase of people, riches,
' and power; and, although no men ought to envy that virtue and
' wisdom in others, which themselves either can, or will not
' practise, but yet rather to commend and admire it; yet,' &c.
&c.—' Name,' writes archbishop Sharp, ' any nation that was
' ever remarkable for justice, for temperance, and severity of
' manners; for piety and religion, *though it was in a wrong way*,
' that did not always thrive, and grow great in the world; and
' that did not always enjoy a plentiful portion of all those things,
' which are accounted to make a nation happy and flourishing.
' And, on the other side, when that nation has declined from its
' former virtue, and grown impious and dissolate in manners, we
' appeal to experience, whether it has not always proportionally sunk
' in its success and good fortune.'

The passages just recited, naturally suggest the other topic to which I allude, which is that of *toleration*; a few words concerning which will terminate the present or second general division of my subject.—It has been said, that " one sect of Christians has killed " more Christians, than all the Pagan persecutions put together." The destruction or exclusion of subjects implies a system which is the very reverse of colozination, by which it is proposed, that men should be multiplied. Those are not likely to have thought much, who do not think variously; as those who are said to think in complete unison, will often be found not to think at all; and if the Deity does not ask of us to think alike, which seems plain from his

not

not taking effectual measures for that purpose, men have no right to enforce an uniformity towards him, in points which do not concern civil society. I am sensible that this discussion will be thought delicate. But those who are afraid of entering upon it, must not expect great success in colonization; for some of the most proper persons to be found in numbers sufficient to begin a colony, are generally sectaries, natives or foreigners. Happily the time appears to approach fast, when the statesman's toleration will be marked in this short catechism: "Does your religion permit "you to plough and manufacture?" "Yes." "Do you acknow-"ledge my authority?" "Yes."—"Be assured then of my pro-"tection. I shall punish loose morals and civil crimes, and keep "you from quarrelling with your neighbours: for the rest, it "belongs to God and your conscience. Shall I, who am a sinner, "judge you!"

ARTICLE X.

Extract from Sir William Temple's Observations on the United Provinces of the Netherlands. Chap. 5 and 6.

I Intend not here to speak of religion at all as a divine, but as a mere secular man.—Whosoever designs the change of religion in a country or government, by any other means than that of a general conversion of the people, or the greatest part of them, designs all the mischiefs to a nation that use to usher in or attend the two greatest distempers of a state, civil war or tyranny; which are violence, oppression, cruelty, rapine, intemperance, injustice; and in short, the miserable effusion of human blood, and the confusion of all laws, orders, and virtues among men. Such consequences as these, I doubt, are something more than the disputed opinions of any man, or any particular assembly of men, can be worth; since the great and general end of all religion, next to men's happiness hereafter, is their happiness here; as appears by the commandments of God, being the best and greatest, moral and civil as well as divine, precepts, that have been given to a nation; and by the rewards proposed to the piety of the Jews, throughout the Old Testament, which were the blessings of this life, as health, length of age, number of children, plenty, peace, or victory.

Now our way to future happiness has been perpetually disputed throughout the world, and must be left at last to the impressions made upon every man's belief and conscience, either by natural or supernatural arguments and means; which impressions, men may disguise or dissemble, but no man can resist. For belief is no more in a man's power, than his stature, or his feature; and he that tells me, I must change my opinion for his, because 'tis the truer and the better, without other arguments that have to me the force of conviction, may as well tell me I must change my grey eyes for others like his that are black, because these are lovelier or more in his esteem. He that tells me, I must inform myself, has reason, if I do it not: but if I endeavour it all that I can and perhaps more than he ever did, and yet still differ from him; and he, that it may be is idle, will have me study on and inform myself better, and so to the end of my life; then I easily understand what he means by informing, which is in short, that I must do it till I come to be of his opinion. If he, that perhaps pursues his pleasures or interests, as much or more than I do; and allows me to have as much good sense as he has in all other matters, tells me I should be of his opinion, but that passion or interest blinds me; unless he can convince me how or where this lies, he is but where he was, only pretends to know me better than I do myself, who cannot imagine, why I should not have as much care of my soul, as he has of his. A man that tells me my opinions are absurd or ridiculous, impertinent or unreasonable, because they differ from his, seems to intend a quarrel, instead of a dispute; and calls me fool or madman with a little more circumstance; though perhaps I pass for one as well in my senses as he, as pertinent in talk, and as prudent in life: yet these are the common civilities in religious argument, of sufficient and conceited men, who talk much of right reason and mean always their own; and make their private imagination the measure of general truth. But such language determines all between us, and the dispute comes to end in three words at last, which it might as well have ended in at first: That he is in the right and I am in the wrong.

The other great end of religion, which is our happiness here, has been generally agreed on by all mankind, as appears in the records of all their laws, as well as all their religions which come to be established by the concurrence of men's customs and opinions *; tho' in the latter they may have been produced by divine impressions or inspirations. For all agree in teaching and commanding, in planting and improving, not only those moral virtues, which conduce to the felicity and tranquility of every private mans life, but also those manners and dispositions that tend to the peace, order and safety of all civil societies and governments among men. Nor could I ever understand, how those who call themselves, and

---

* Fiunt diversæ respublicæ ex civium moribus; qui, quocunque fluxerint, cætera secum rapiunt. Plat. de Rep.

the world usually calls *religious men*, come to put so great weight upon those points of belief which men never have agreed in, and so little upon those of virtue and morality in which they have hardly ever disagreed. Nor, why a state should venture the subversion of their peace and their order, which are certain goods and so universally esteemed, for their propogation of uncertain or contested opinions.

One of the great causes of the first revolt in the low countries appeared to be the oppression of men's consciences, or persecution in their liberties, their estates and their lives, upon pretence of religion. And this at a time, *when there seemed to be a conspiring disposition in most countries of Christendom, to seek the reformation of some abuses,* grown in the doctrine and discipline of the church, either by the rust of time, by negligence, or by human inventions, passions and interests.

Another circumstance was the general liberty and ease, not only in point of conscience, but all others that serve to the commodiousness and quiet of life; every man following his own way, minding his own business, and little enquiring into other mens; which, I suppose, happened by so great concourse of people of several nations, different religion and customs, as left nothing strange or new; and by the general humour, bent all upon industry, whereas curiosity is only proper to idle men. Besides it has ever been the great principle of their state, running through all their provinces and cities, even with emulation, to make their country the common refuge of all miserable men; from whose protection, hardly any alliances, treaties, or interests, have ever been able to divert or remove them. So as during the great dependence this state had upon France, in the time of Henry IV. all the persons disgraced at that court, or banished that country, made it their common retreat; nor could the state ever be prevailed with, by any instances of the French ambassadors, to refuse them the use and liberty of common life and air, under the protection of their government. This firmness in the state has been one of the circumstances, that has invited so many unhappy men out of all their neighbourhood, and indeed from most parts of Europe, to shelter themselves from the blows of justice, or of fortune.

ARTICLE XI.

Arguments extracted from the Pamphlet intituled " the Rights of the " Dissenters to a compleat Toleration asserted." 2d Edit. 1789.

THE Dissenters of the present day do not contend for establishment, nor is disaffection to the subsisting government, in the least connected with any of the religious distinctions among them

them. Whether the Test is defended as a security to church or state, they may assert their right to be restored to the rank of citizens, for they hold opinions hostile to neither.—With respect to their sentiments on civil government, they are precisely the same as the members of the church of England are understood to profess. They are the friends of civil liberty; they assert the principles on which the glorious Revolution was founded, and which placed the House of Hanover on the throne. The charge of disaffection to the present government is inconsistent with these principles, and unsupported by any part of their conduct. They have run great risks, and with greater unanimity, to establish and preserve it, than any other set of men whatever. During the reign of Charles the Second, the small remains of liberty in England were chiefly preserved and cherished by them. They resisted, with effect, the arbitrary designs of Charles, and his unfortunate brother, when their own immediate interest would have led them to unconditional submission; they joined cordially in the Revolution; and exposed themselves to the resentment of a bigotted princess, and an infatuated people, to secure the accession of the House of Hanover. This, and more they generously did, without making any terms for themselves. The unkind returns they met with never diminished their attachment to that family, nor damped their ardour in the cause of liberty. In two rebellions, the Dissenters, without the exception of a single individual, shewed a steady attachment to the present government; while within the pale of the church were found the zealous champions of passive obedience and the Stuart race.— Against facts so notorious, the Dissenters cannot be accused of disaffection to the present government.

The experience of more than one hundred and twenty years has sufficiently shewn, that in the opinions of the Dissenters there is nothing dangerous to the established church. Their exertions preserved that church in the reign of Charles the Second, and they were instrumental in bringing about the Revolution, when its destruction was nearly accomplished. And let it not be forgotten, that at the conclusion of the reign of Queen Anne, they strenuously opposed the intrigues of the court, to give its supremacy to a popish prince, in exclusion of the House of Brunswick—Are the persons who gave up their own interest to secure the national church, to be suspected of designs to destroy it? and can that church need a weapon of defence against such Dissenters? against Dissenters, who for upwards of a century have rendered it every assistance in their power, and preserved it more than once from ruin?

The entire extinction of the sect of Presbyterians in England, who are now become independents as to church government, and the strictness with which multitudes of the Dissenters adhere to the doctrines of the church, as stated in the Thirty-nine Articles, (a strictness far exceeding that with which they are accepted in general by the clergy) these two circumstances, I say, may serve to compose the apprehensions of the clergy as to any danger from acceding to the present claims of the Dissenting laity.

But there is another style of argument on this subject, even yet more convincing than the foregoing, drawn from the conduct of the protestant dissenters settled in the different parts of north America. After the power of England ceased in that country, they have shewn in the northern and middle Colonies, that they have been falsely accused of objections to the introduction of bishops. Those states which mostly wanted bishops, from having the espiscopalian system prevalent among them, namely, the more southern Colonies, are precisely those which have been most backward in procuring the establishment of bishops.—The states most filled with dissenters are the states also among them which have been most liberal respecting Test laws, which, it must be observed, are confined in general (where they exist) to persons seated in the legislature, and do not extend to inferior offices, one or two states excepted.—The declaration of the state of Virginia respecting religious liberty is a masterpiece, deserving record in letters of gold. And the 6th article of the plan of the new constitution for the United States in America, made in 1787, provides, ‘ that no religious Test shall ever ‘ be required as a qualification to any office or public trust under ‘ the United States.'

It is true, that some of the dissenters in North America were formerly intolerant; but Dr. Franklin, in a letter written in 1772, expressly to favour the application of the dissenting ministers for relief from subscription to religious articles, has given the *explanation*, which it is impossible to avoid reciting here.—‘ If we look back' (says he) ‘ into history for ‘ the character of the present sects in christianity, we shall ‘ find few that have not, in their turns, been persecutors ‘ and complainers of persecution. The primitive christians ‘ thought persecution extremely wrong in the pagans, but prac- ‘ tised it one on another. The first protestants of the church of ‘ England blamed persecution in the Romish church, but prac- ‘ tised it against the puritans: these found it wrong in the bishops, ‘ but fell into the same practice both in Old and New England.— ‘ To *account* for this we should remember, that the doctrine of
‘ toleration

' toleration was not then *known*, or had not prevailed in the world.
' Persecution was therefore not so much the fault of the sect, as of
' the times. It was not in those days deemed wrong in *itself*;
' the general opinion was only, that those who are in error ought
' not to persecute the truth ; but the possessors of truth were in
' the right to persecute error, in order to destroy it. Thus every
' sect believing itself possessed of all truth, and that every tenet dif-
' fering from theirs was error, conceived that when the power was in
' their hands, persecution was a duty required of them by that God
' whom they supposed to be offended with heresy. — By degrees,
' more moderate and more *modest* sentiments have taken place in
' the christian world ; and among protestants particularly, all dis-
' claim persecution, none vindicate, and few practise it. We
' should then cease to reproach each other with what was done by
' our ancestors, but judge of the present character of sects and
' churches by their *present conduct* only.

' Now to determine on the justice of this charge against the
' *present* dissenters, particularly those in America, let us consider
' the following facts. They went from England to establish a new
' country for themselves at their own expence, where they might
' enjoy the free exercise of their religion in their own way. When
' they had purchased the territory of the natives, they granted
' the lands out in townships, requiring for it neither purchase-
' money nor quit-rent, but this condition only to be complied
' with; that the freeholders should support a gospel-minister
' (meaning probably one of the then governing sects) and a free-
' school within the township. * * * But in process of time * * *
' some turning to the church of England, * * * objections were
' made to the payment of a tax appropriated to the support of a
' church they disapproved of and had forsaken. The civil magis-
' trates, however, continued for a time to collect and apply the
' tax, according to the original laws which remained in force ; and
' they did it the more freely, as thinking it just and equitable that
' the holders of lands should pay what was contracted to be paid
' when they were granted, as the only consideration for the grant.
' * * * But the practice being clamoured against by the Episco-
' palians as persecution, the Legislature of Massachusets Bay, near
' thirty years since, passed an Act for their relief; requiring indeed
' the tax to be paid as usual, but directing that the several sums
' levied from members of the church of England, should be paid
' over to the minister of that church with whom such members
' usually attended divine worship ; which minister had power given
' him to receive, and on occasion *to recover the same by law.* * * *

' And now let us see how this persecution account stands be-
' tween the parties.

"In

In *New England*, where the legislative bodies are almost to a man dissenters from the church of England,	In *Old England*.
1. There is no test to prevent churchmen holding offices.	1. Dissenters are excluded from all offices of profit and honour.
2. The sons of churchmen have the full benefit of the universities.	2. The benefits of education in the universities are appropriated to the sons of churchmen.
3. The taxes for support of public worship, when paid by churchmen, are given to the episcopal minister.	3. The clergy of the dissenters receive none of the tythes paid by their people, who must be at the additional charge of maintaining their own separate worship."

The Northern States, it must be added, are very rigid; but in what? not in enforcing belief, or contribution, or submission to any established sect; but in carrying into strict execution all laws for due observance of the sabbath, and against profane swearing, &c. which as every justice of peace knows, make part of the laws of this country, though certainly very little enforced. These measures do not go to prohibit this or the other sect; but rather to second the endeavours of its ministers for the propagation of each. Accordingly we find, in the late Declaration of Rights which formed the foundation of the new Massachusets constitution: 'That in this state *every* denomination of Christians, demeaning themselves peaceably and as good subjects of the commonwealth, shall be *equally* under the protection of the law; and no subordination of one sect to another shall *ever* be established by law.'

Certain it is, that no countries under the sun, shew more indulgences to variety in religious opinions than the United States of North America; and since so large a majority of their citizens are Dissenters, nothing can be more clear than that the modern disposition of Dissenters, as Dissenters is not intolerant.

It remains therefore for the clergy to decide, as far as respects their influence and exertions, whether or not they will accede to the request of the Dissenting Laity upon the present occasion. By acceding, they see how little risque they run. By not acceding, they will have one difficulty more to contend with, in the situation into which they are brought, by their own decline in strict manners and official diligence on the one side, and by the change of opinion and of disposition in the laity of all descriptions and sects on the other. The Dissenters are not perhaps an important body in themselves; but as furnishing a *measure*, by which to judge of the Christian spirit of the clergy, their case may in the event produce an impression upon the minds of *others*, who are not Dissenters.—There are two ways of treating difficulties of this sort: the one is, of resisting every change, which is in other words, a *trial of strength*;

strength; the other is, of giving way and compounding upon some points, that the call for strength being thus made less, there may be sufficient for supporting the remaining points. The public opinion is changing fast on many subjects; and shall the clergy wait till things accumulate, or redress so much, as to make people *contented* under what remains; shall they open sluices to carry off a part of the approaching tide, or oppose the dam of ancient prejudices to stem the whole? —The question respects themselves, more than the dissenters or the public; for who have most at stake?— This is not the language of insolence, but of friendship, good order, tranquillity, and religion.

The diminution in number of the dissenters, since they have been relieved from the penal laws, prevents a possibility of mischief to the established church from repealing the test acts. Their body would not be increased, and the churchmen would still form a most prodigious majority; they would still far out-number all the sects of nonconformists *put together*. That majority, which gave the church of England her existence as an established church, and still supports her, is not likely to be diminished by her shewing regard to the rights of others; especially as it will remove one principal objection of the dissenters, namely, that she is not enough tolerant.— But should the establishment become the minority, compared with *the whole body* of dissenters, (which becomes daily less likely to happen,) they could never unite their discordant interests in an attack upon it; but would prefer the enjoyment of their present portion of liberty, to the chance of being more at ease under each other.

The repeal of the Test laws would not exclude a single churchman, or put the dissenters in possession of any one public office, but would only render them eligible to such as might be offered.

If questions of late have been agitated concerning tythes, has it not been by the landed interest? or if concerning ecclesiastical courts or powers, has it not been in the legislature only? Have not the dissenters been silent as a body, except when attacked, or as mere controversial writers on points of doctrine, and not of power or possessions?—And on the other hand, have they not fought the general cause of religion against deists and atheists, and, by the confession of many dignitaries in the church, (who have made the circumstance matter of reproach to their own inferior clergy) have they have not done it with great zeal and effect, and has not this ultimately strengthened the establishment?—In short, they have founded their chief comfort in tranquillity; and manifested every mark of satisfaction in the civil and religious constitution of their country, their own hardships excepted?—Their ministers have made no ill use of the enlarged toleration lately granted; nor will

their

their laymen of that now fought for. The church may therefore rest assured, that the dissenters are never likely to attack *their* rights, unless it should be indispensable for the restoration of their own; and that the most effectual way of disarming them as foes is by making them friends.

That nation is the most strong (*cæteris paribus*) where the people are most united; and that is the most weak where intestine divisions rage with greatest violence. Of course the relative strength of this island is infinitely greater than before the union; for by that great event every cause of dispute between the two sister kingdoms was removed, and both were united in one common interest, instead of weakening each other by perpetual jealousies and broils. For the same reason the executive power has of late acquired a vast accession of strength. The two first princes of the house of Hanover were called upon, almost without respite, to punish plots, to quiet rebellions, and to repel open attacks upon the crown. But how widely different the present reign! His Majesty has for thirty years swayed the British sceptre in perfect peace at home, at least from the factions which before were wont to agitate the empire; the claims of a foreign Pretender to the throne are worn out and forgotten; the nonconformists have been daily diminishing in numbers, and those that are left have, by lenity and kindness, been much conciliated to the national church. So that his Majesty presides over a people more powerful and united than any of his predecessors; and the kingdom enjoys a tranquillity which has not been known for centuries in Britain; for the parties of politicians now subsisting make but a small figure in a national view, and secure, rather than shake, both throne and constitution. If the ministers of the church, therefore, fancy themselves to be *allied* to the state, they must feel that their establishment grows more firm, as the throne becomes more stable; and an attention to their own interest, as well as the precepts of christianity, should induce them to strengthen this union, and to render this tranquillity as permanent as possible. To accomplish these objects, no means can be devised so effectual and so certain as the removal of every cause of uneasiness on account of religious matters, more especially when it will be followed with no danger to the state or their own religion.

It will be a little singular, that when deism increases, when taxes grow burthensome, when the press is open, when a liberal spirit is rising by a sort of common consent in the public, and in the government of every nation in Europe, that the clergy of this country, who have such large civil privileges at stake, besides their ecclesiastical ones, together with immense revenues, (not collected in a mode to give perfect content, nor yet distributed among their own members in a way to give a due subsistence or satisfaction to all,) it will be singular, if, under such peculiar circumstances, the dignitaries of the church should oppose the course of policy and justice in favour of the dissenters, who have so many pleas in their favour; so little terror to inspire, when duly treated; and whose cause will plead eloquently for them in the present age, were they themselves to remain silent, which yet cannot be expected. Those are wise who have preventive wisdom; and, taking into consideration the circumstances just stated on the one hand, and the little to be gained by an obstinate resistance to reform in favour of so small a body of persons, whose case can be drawn into no precedent if relieved, there can be no doubt on *which* side preventive wisdom lies.—It is not a selection of a few characters, and a few writers, from among the whole body of dissenters, that can justify any harsh conclusion as to the whole of them, and much less any harsh measure. They are to be judged of generally, for a course of time, and with the eyes of a statesman; and the more especially, as a refusal of their requests will produce no change in the individuals complained of, who, if they offend at all, must be acknowledged to offend even under the present system of severity and ill-will.

With one observation more, addressed to those who retain the notion that the bare existence of nonconformity is an evil to a state, I shall conclude this part of the argument.—I will not pay these persons so ill a compliment, as to suppose, that a little reflection would not cure them of this prepossession. The religious, as well as political system, benefits by a little variety of opinion, and by an opposition of characters; and the many able defences of natural and revealed religion, and the many excellent moral writings proceeding from the dissenters, are a proof that they have offered a positive advantage to the church, by confirming that grand *basis* on which it is ultimately built. Their writings also have, in the opinion of many of the clergy, helped to liberalize the church itself; which, if there had been no sects existing, would probably have retained many of those absurd tenets which prevailed a century ago. The greater strictness of education among the more rigid sectaries, is another advantage arising from Nonconformity, and hence chiefly manufactures and commerce have been found to prosper so much in the hands of sectaries, where they have not been too severely treated; and hence likewise their riches, and, as a consequence of their riches and softened manners, their frequent reunion, in a few generations, with the establishment of the country where they are found.—But such is the propensity of mankind to variety of opinions, that were there no sects now among us, they would soon start up out of the church itself, of which certain respectable favourers of Socinianism

have

have furnished a signal example; and persecution is not only a bad measure in itself for preventing it, but it is too late in the day to use it*.

It has been found in all countries, and been felt by none more forcibly than England, that lenient measures are best calculated to diminish the number of Nonconformists. It is an approved maxim in religious politics, that by taking away the distinctions which separate them from the establishment, they are most likely to be joined to it. They are united *as a body*, only under persecution; and the instant they are suffered to form one mass indiscriminately with the rest of the People, they cease to be formidable. Deprive them of that zeal which leads martyrs to the stake, and they lose the power to resist temptation. The proud and haughty spirit which bears undaunted the infliction of corporal punishment, or of death itself, submits quietly to the suggestions of interest, and the allurements of the world. One of the most grievous oppressions under which the Dissenters now labour, is their exclusion from offices; and this mark of reproach is the chief circumstance, which distinguishes them from their fellow citizens. Rapid as we know the decrease of numbers among them to have been since the Revolution, some even of their own body have been of opinion, that if they had been restored at that period to *all* their civil rights, it must have been much greater; and such have dreaded

* 'Religious freedom (which is an essential assistant to trade) appears daily gaining strength and popularity; its chief obstacles lying in the bigotry or habitual bad politics of established clergymen, and in the complaisance of timid or subtle statesmen in their favour. In return for the contributions made by men of other religious persuasions to their permanent support, the established clergy in general, throughout Europe, have not only encouraged the exclusion of such persons from civil offices, (although these persons contribute to the support of civil offices also) but they have usually in the first instance pleaded even against indulging them in the privilege of cultivating their religion in private.—The clergy beyond all men, one might suppose, ought to know, that religion is a belief and not a form, a personal and not a state concern; and that though the state may derive benefits from its prevalence, it ought never to prescribe the particular modes of it. But since experience has shewn that none have been more ready than the clergy to interfere in the private concerns of other men with their Creator, and that no associated body of men is so slow in reforming its errors as their own: it is time that the civil power should interfere and decisively abolish every thing favoring of religious persecution; confining the power of the clergy to the discipline of their own followers subject to their own consent —As to the sectaries of modern Europe, I conceive that facts and authorities prove it to be very beneficial to a country, that a part of its inhabitants should be of this description; or at least if sectaries have no positive advantage to recommend them it is certainly impolitic where sectaries occur, either to expel or to oppress them; and not less impolitic to deny them shelter, when they seek admittance from foreign parts in numbers too small to create danger; especially where they possess wealth, skill, or extensive commercial connections. The religious forbearance that daily and mutually increases among men of all persuasions, constantly lessens the probability of serious disputes arising from different religions being professed in the same neighbourhood; especially where the state applies a due authority in support of the general peace.

the removal of the Sacramental Test, as the most fatal circumstance that could happen to their interest.—If this argument is not sufficient to prove, that the Dissenters will be gradually extinguished by the grant of their wishes (an event which a statesman, and the wiser clergy, would have to view with some regret); still it will be sufficient to prove, that no *new* dangers to the state, or church, are to be expected to result in consequence of its increasing their numbers, their want of tractability, or their power.

The experience of ancient and modern times has taught us that the prelates of the church have a commanding influence; and it is unfortunately true that upon several occasions, and in different reigns, they have prevented the favourable dispositions of those in power from operating to the relief of Protestant Dissenters. The maxims of persecution formerly taught by the church of England, have been disavowed by most of its present teachers, *as individuals*. They would be ashamed to have it believed, that every modern archbishop is a *Laud*, and every Homily full of standard truth. But the tenets *of the church* itself remain the same, and would authorize the persecution of Nonconformists to the utmost extremity. Restore the *power* of burning heretics (which was not taken away till the end of Charles the Second's reign) and in perfect consistency with the principals of this Protestant church, its Courts may even now confer the crown of martyrdom *. The state has retracted in open day many of the errors of its conduct towards sectaries; but the church has not in a body disavowed a single one. Thus modern prelates, as such, appear in support of tenets which, as individuals, they utterly disclaim.—But why do they submit to this degradation of the episcopal character?—because of the danger of innovation. A prey to imaginary fears, they dare not give up the persecuting doctrines of their church, even though they openly disapprove them. The bishops therefore, thus interested in supporting clerical usurpa-

---

* In the provincial synod of the province of Canterbury, William Sawtre was convicted of being a relapsed heretic, in the second year of the reign of Henry the Fourth, and the king in parliament issued a writ to commit him to the flames. This was a roundabout way of doing the business, and therefore, in the same year, the Prelates and Clergy petitioned parliament, that wherever the diocesan or his commissaries should convict a person of heresy, and he should refuse to abjure, or having abjured should afterwards relapse, the secular power might be called in, without the interference of provincial synods, parliament, or king. Their request was granted, and their power to dye the earth with blood was exercised in the reign of Elizabeth; and under James the First, Wightman and Legate perished at the stake. Since that time, the doctrines of the church have not undergone the smallest alteration. The power of burning hereticks was taken away in the year 1676, but the spiritual courts may still punish them " by excom-" munication; deprivation, degradation, and other ecclesiastical censures not extending " to death."

tions, are the last persons by whom a minister should be advised in a question concerning toleration. If the change be in itself good, it is his duty to remove their apprehensions, to assure their minds, and to pursue his measures.—The bishops opposed the application for relief of the Dissenting ministers. Twice that bill passed the House of Commons, and twice it was thrown out in the House of Lords; and at both times, *all the bishops* who were present, or sent their proxies, voted against it: but happily the minister of the day was not infected by their unmanly fears; his Majesty gave his hearty concurrence to the application; and at length the bishops, ashamed of terrors which were confined to their own bench, and convinced by the arguments used in the debates, ceased their opposition.

Under the administrations of Cardinals Richlieu and Mazarin, (says the same author) Protestants in France held offices both civil and military; and the latter intrusted Turenne, who was a Protestant, with an army against the Prince of Condé, not only a Protestant, but his relation. Schomberg, Ruvigni, and many others, were placed in offices of high trust and consequence, under Lewis the Fourteenth, till the revocation of the edict of Nantz. But to come down to later times, Marshal Saxe was employed by Lewis the XVth to oppose a Protestant army; and the court of France has, within these few years, raised Mr. Necker, a Protestant also, (originally a private citizen of Geneva) to the head of the finances. His zeal and public spirit, as well as the example of other Protestants, have deeply impressed this truth upon the minds of his fellow subjects, *that a Dissenter from the established religion of a country may be a true friend to its interests.* The wisdom and ability with which he has discharged the trust reposed in him, have reflected infinite honour upon himself; and the principles he has fostered may, at some future period, make Great-Britain regret, that a Popish country should disdain to be shackled by maxims of religion intolerant as her own.—The popularity attending most of the above promotions, is a clear proof that the kingdom of France was influenced by some liberality, as well as its Princes.

In the Imperial armies, and in some of the Imperial dominions Protestants have often been raised to high offices and commands, and many are at this day in their hands. The attention lately paid by the Emperor to the interests of his Protestant subjects, leaves no room to doubt that the remaining distinctions between them and the Catholics are dying away.

The Empress of Russia too has not scrupled to employ in the highest offices, persons dissenting from the established religion of
her

her dominions. The naval power of Ruffia will be a lafting memorial of the fervices of Admiral Greig.

On the other hand, the practice of the countries in Europe, profeffing the Proteftant religion, proves, that a Sacramental Teft is not *neceffary* for the fecurity of an eftablifhed church, for it is unknown to them all. And there is no example in hiftory, of any of their churches being in danger, merely from the admiffion of fectaries into office.

ARTICLE XII.

Lord Mansfield's Opinion on Toleration, with a Tranflation of the Paffages which his Lordfhip referred to in Prefident De Thou.

WHEN the cafe of Mr. Evans, a diffenter, fined by the city of London for refufing to ferve the office, which required the taking of the facramental teft as its qualification, was heard before the Houfe of Lords, Lord Mansfield expreffed himfelf in the following ftrain of eloquence:—" What bloodfhed and confufion
" have been occafioned from the reign of Henry IV. when the firft
" penal ftatutes were enacted, down to the Revolution, in this king-
" dom, by laws made to force confcience! There is nothing cer-
" tainly more unreafonable, more inconfiftent with the rights of
" human nature, more contrary to the fpirit and precepts of the
" Chriftian religion, more iniquitous and unjuft, more impolitic;
" than perfecution. It is againft natural religion, revealed religion,
" and found policy."

" Sad experience, and a large mind, taught that great man, the
" Prefident de Thou, this doctrine:—Let any man read the many
" admirable things, which, though a papift, he hath dared to ad-
" vance upon the fubject, in the dedication of his hiftory to Henry
" IV. of France, (which I never read without rapture) and he will
" be fully convinced, not only how cruel, but how *impolitic* it is
" to perfecute for religious opinions. I am forry that of late his
" countrymen have begun to open their eyes, fee their error, and
" adopt his fentiments. I fhould not have broke my heart, (I
" hope I may fay fo without breach of Chriftian charity) if France
" had continued to cherifh the Jefuits, and to perfecute the Hu-
" guenots[*]. There was no occafion for this end to revoke the

---

[*] Lord Mansfield *then* fpoke of France as an *arbitrary* monarchy, which in proportion to its power threatened the liberties of Europe.

" edict

"edict of Nantes; the Jesuits needed only to have advised a plan
"similar to what is contended for in the present case: Make a law
"to render them incapable of offices; make another to punish
"them (for it is admitted on all hands, that the defendant in the
"cause before your Lordships is prosecuteable for taking the office
"upon him): if they accept, punish, if they refuse, punish: if
"they say yes, punish, if they say no, punish. My Lords, this is
"a most exquisite dilemma, from which there is no escaping; it is
"a trap a man cannot get out of; it is as bad persecution as that
"of Procrustes: if they are too short stretch them; if they are
"too long, lop them. Small would have been their consolation to
"have been gravely told, the edict of Nantes is kept inviolable,
"you have the full benefit of that Act of Toleration; you may
"take the Sacrament in your own way with impunity; you are
"not compelled to go to mass. Was this case but told in the city
"of London as a proceeding in France, how would they exclaim
"against the jesuitical distinction! And yet in truth it comes from
"themselves: The Jesuits never thought of it: when they meant
"to persecute, their Act of Toleration, the edict of Nantes, was
"repealed."—Appendix to Furneaux's Letters to Judge Blackstone.

Translation of the Passages in De Thou's Address to Henry the IVth. of France, alluded to by Lord Mansfield.

Experience sufficiently teaches us that the sword, the faggot, exile and proscriptions, are better calculated to irritate than to heal a disease, which, having its source in the mind, cannot be relieved by remedies that act only on the body. The most efficacious means are found doctrine and repeated instructions, which make a ready impression when inculcated with mildness. Every thing else bows to the sovereign authority of the magistrates and the prince; but religion alone is not to be commanded.

What the Stoics have so vauntingly ascribed to their philosophy, religion has a higher claim to. Torments appear trivial to those who are animated by religious zeal: the firmness with which it inspires them, deadens the sentiment of pain; nothing they are obliged to suffer for its sake, however aggravated, occasions them surprize; the knowledge of their own strength enables them to bear every thing, while they are persuaded that the grace of God supports them. Though the executioner appear before them, and exhibit to their view the sword and the stake, their minds are undaunted; and regardless of the sufferings that are preparing for them, they are attentive solely to their duty: all their happiness is in themselves, and external objects make upon them but a feeble impression.

If

If Epicurus, whose system has been so much decried by other philosophers, has said of the sage, that if he were shut up in the brazen bull of Phalaris, he would not fail to declare: "this fire "affects me not, it is not I that burn:" do we imagine that less courage was conspicuous in those who by various torments were put to death a century ago, or that less will be displayed by future martyrs, if persecution be continued? What was said and done by one of them, when he was fastened to the stake in order to be burned, is worthy our notice. Being upon his knees, he began to sing a psalm, which the smoke and the flame could scarcely interrupt; and as the executioner, for fear of terrifying him, lighted the fire behind, he turned and said: "come and kindle it before "me: if fire could have terrified me, I should not be here; it "depended on myself alone to avoid it."

It is in vain, therefore, by torments to attempt to suppress the ardour of those who are desirous of introducing novelties in religion. This tends only to inspire constancy and enable them to exert the greater efforts. From the ashes of those who have been put to death, new zealots spring up; as their numbers increase, their patience transforms itself into rage; from suppliants they become importunate and confident claimants, and if at first they fled from punishment, they no longer hesitate to have recourse to arms.

This has happened during forty years in France, and since in the Low Countries. Every thing there is at length reduced to such extremities, that the hope would be futile of stopping the progress of the evil by the sacrifice of a few victims, which in the commencement might have succeeded. Now that it is diffused through whole nations and people, composing the greater part of Europe, the sword of the magistrate can no longer be employed; the sword of the word of God ought to be the sole weapon; and those who are no longer to be compelled, should be gently attracted by moderate conversations and amicable discussions.

Thus it is that in Germany, in England, and in France, it is not possible to say which has suffered most, public tranquillity or religion. Schism arose and obtained strength from the indolence and negligence of those, who might and ought to have found a remedy for it.

I would not be understood by this, as wishing to revive a question which has been so often discussed: whether heretics ought to be punished with death? This would neither be suited to the times nor to my profession. My design is to show that those princes have acted with prudence and agreeably to the maxims of the primitive church, who have terminated religious wars by mildness rather than by force of arms, though upon disadvantageous conditions.

The protestants who diminished both in number and credit in times of peace, have always increased when we were divided and
at

at war. Those who govern the state therefore have committed a fatal error, whenever instigated by ambition, by an indiscreet zeal or the desire of rendering themselves necessary during a state of troubles, they have lighted up a cruel war; a war that has so frequently been terminated and revived again under auspices ruinous to the country, and highly detrimental to religion.

But why should we reason upon the subject? the thing speaks for itself. The protestants, in consequence of the troubles in which we were involved, having taken many of our towns, which were given back by a peace in 1563, was it to be wondered at that tranquility should suddenly be restored? How sweet was this calm, which lasted four years, to the virtuous mind, and how salutary at the same time to religion which was secured from danger by the laws! But by a proceeding inimical to our happiness, we became tired of the public safety which the law had established, and spurning at the councils of peace, we engaged in a new war, equally fatal both to its authors and the people.

Francois Baudouin d'Arras wrote a treatise in French, which proved by solid argument that religious differences might more easily be appeased by amicable discussion and leaving to each party the enjoyment of its right, than by violence and force of arms; that if compulsory means were continued, he foresaw that the protestants whose strength at present was inconsiderable, and who were besides divided among themselves, would reunite, and that at last disputes about words, would lead to arms and a revolt.

You have revoked all the edicts which your royal predecessor, contrary to his inclinations, published against the protestants and against yourself. After a glorious peace, both with your own subjects and with foreign nations, you have by a third edict, confirmed the edicts already established in favour of protestants; you have secured to them their habitations, their property, and their honour; you have even advanced some of them to the first dignities of the state, with the hope that, hatred and animosity subsiding, the unanimity prescribed by your edicts would more speedily take place, that the minds of the public would regain their former serenity, and that the cloud of their passions being dispelled, they would be more capable of chusing what was best in religion; I mean, what would be found most conformable to antiquity.

As these considerations, Sire, as well as my own experience and your Majesty's example, have convinced me that I ought to contribute every thing in my power to the peace of the church, I have endeavoured not to speak ill of any person. I have mentioned the Protestants with esteem, particularly such as have distinguished themselves by their learning. On the other hand, I have not dissembled the defects of those of our own party, persuaded, as many

very

very virtuous men are, that we deceive ourselves if we imagine that our own vices and scandals do not contribute more than the malice and artifice of sectaries, to the extending and strengthening the many and various heresies which at present disturb the world.

I conceive that the true way of remedying both the immoralities of the opposite party, as well as our own vices, is to banish from the state every species of base traffic; to recompence merit; to chuse for the guides of the church, men of learning and piety, of an exemplary life, and a prudence and moderation that has been put to the proof; to raise to the first honours of the state, not worthless persons who have no other claim than favour or wealth, but those who have rendered themselves respectable by an established integrity, by a solid piety, by a true disinterestedness, in a word, by the sole recommendation of their virtue. Upon no other plan can peace be rendered durable. Nations must unavoidably fall to ruin, if in the distribution of offices the sovereigns cannot distinguish the honest from the depraved; and if, according to the ancient proverb, "they let the hornets devour what belongs to the bees."

Vices observe no measure and keep within no bounds. Their progress is like that of bodies which roll down a precipice; nothing can stop them but their own destruction. But virtue (as Simonides expresses it) resembles a cube; it resists, by the firmness of its base, all the revolutions of the world and of fortune. As it accommodates itself to different states of life, it keeps the mind of man in a state of liberty that nothing can destroy; it is satisfied with itself, and self-sufficient to every thing. Since then it is of so great utility, the state that properly esteems it, and bestows upon it the honours to which it is entitled, will be able, without increasing the public treasury, and even by relieving the burthens of the people, to confer liberalities on its meritorious citizens *.

ARTICLE XIII.

Extracts from the Sixtieth and Sixty-fifth of the Persian Letters of Montesquieu.

THOU askest me if there are any jews in France? Know, that throughout the world wherever there is money, there are jews. Thou inquirest what they do here? The very same they do in Persia: nothing more resembles a jew in Asia, than a jew in Europe. They show among the christians, as among us, an invincible obstinacy for their religion, which they carry to the

* Both President de Thou and Mr. Turgot have been very successful in exhibiting passages in favour of religious liberty.

height

height of folly. The religion of the jews is an old trunk which hath produced two branches, which have covered all the earth, I mean chriſtianity and mahometaniſm: or rather, it is a mother who hath brought forth two daughters, who have covered her with a thouſand wounds; for, with reſpect to religion, its neareſt friends are its greateſt enemies. But as ill as ſhe has been treated by theſe, ſhe doth not ceaſe to glory in having produced them; ſhe ſerves herſelf of both to encompaſs the whole world; whilſt on her own part, her venerable age embraces all ages. The jews conſider themſelves as the ſource of all holineſs, and the origin of all religion: they, on the other hand, look upon us as hereticks who have changed the law, or rather as rebellious jews. If the change had been gradually effected, they think they might have been eaſily ſeduced; but as it was ſuddenly changed and in a violent manner, as they can point out the day and the hour of the birth of the one and the other, they are offended at finding us reckoning our religion by ages, and therefore adhere firmly to a religion, not preceded in antiquity by even the world itſelf. They never enjoyed in Europe a calm equal to the preſent. Chriſtians begin to lay aſide that intolerating ſpirit which formerly influenced them. Spain hath experienced the bad conſequence of having expelled the jews, and France of having worried the chriſtians, whoſe faith differed a little from that of the prince. They are now ſenſible that a zeal for the progreſs of religion is different from that attachment which ought to be preſerved towards her. It is to be wiſhed that our muſſulmans would think as rationally upon this ſubject as the Chriſtians, that we might, in good earneſt, make peace between Hali and Abubeker, and leave to God the care of deciding the pretenſions of theſe holy prophets.

Thou knoweſt Mirza, that ſome of the miniſters of Cha Soliman, had formed a deſign to oblige all the Armenians in Perſia to quit the kingdom, or to embrace Mahometaniſm, from a conceit that our empire would be always defiled as long as ſhe protected theſe infidels in her boſom. This had finiſhed the Perſian greatneſs, if, on this occaſion blind devotion had been liſtened to. It is unknown how this affair failed. Neither thoſe who made the propoſal, nor thoſe who rejected it were ſenſible of the conſequences: chance did the office of reaſon and policy, and ſaved the empire from a greater danger than it would have gone through from the loſs of a battle, and of two cities. By baniſhing the Armenians, it is ſuppoſed, they would have rooted out, at once, all the traders, and very near all the artificers in the kingdom. I am certain that the great Cha Abbas, would rather have cut off both his arms, than have ſigned ſuch an order; and he would have been of opinion

hion, that by thus sending to the Mogul, and the other kings of the Indies, the most industrious of his subjects, he had given them half his dominions. The persecution which our Mahometan zealots exercised against the Guebres, obliged them to remove in multitudes into the Indies; and deprived Persia of that people so much given to tillage, and who alone by their industry, were in a way to get the better of the sterility of our lands. There remained but one thing more for bigotry to do, that was to destroy industry; and then the empire had fallen of itself, and with it, as a necessary consequence, that very religion it wanted to render so flourishing.—If we could reason without prejudice, I know not, Mirza, but it may be good for a state, that there should be several religions in it. It is observable, that the members of the tolerated religions commonly make themselves more useful to their country than those of the established religion; because, being excluded from all honours, they can only render themselves considerable by their opulence; they are led to acquire this by their industry, and to embrace the most toilsome employments in the society. Besides, as all religions contain precepts useful to society, it is good that they should be observed with zeal. Now what is there more capable of animating this zeal than a multiplicity of religions? They are rivals who never forgive any thing. This jealousy descends to individuals; each keeps upon his guard, and is cautious of doing any thing that may dishonour his party, and expose it to the contempt and unforgiving censures of the opposite party. Accordingly it has always been observed, that a new sect introduced into a state, hath been the most certain means of reforming all the abuses of the old one. It signifies nothing to say, that it is not the prince's interest to permit several religions in his kingdom. Though all the sects in the world were to get together in it, it would not be any prejudice to it; for there is not one that doth not enjoin obedience, and that doth not preach up submission.—I acknowledge that history is full of religious wars: but we must take care to observe, it was not the multiplicity of religions that produced these wars, it was the intolerating spirit which animated that which thought she had the power of governing. It was the spirit of proselytism, which the Jews contracted from the Egyptians, and which from them hath passed, like an epidemic and popular disease, to Mahometans and Christians. It is in short, the spirit of enthusiasm; the progress of which can be considered only as a total eclipse of human reason. For indeed if there was nothing of inhumanity in forcing the conscience of another, though there did not arise from it any of those bad effects which spring from it by thousands, it would be folly to advise it. He who would have me change my religion, no doubt, desires me to do so, because he would not change his own if he was forced to it: he yet thinks it strange, that I will not do a thing which he himself would not do, perhaps, for the empire of the world. ARTICLE

ARTICLE XIV.

Substance of Mr. Necker's Opinion respecting religious Liberty, taken from his Work on the Importance of Religious Opinions.

RELIGION is not the natural origin of wars and troubles; for it inculcates charity, which gets the better of intolerance. In any event it has never been the sole agent of mischief; and if we are to object to it on account of its wars, what shall we say to commerce, which has been the source of like evils? Besides, these mischiefs are now brought to an end; and shall we throw down the building the moment it becomes to be settled on its base?— After some remarks of this sort, M. Necker proceeds to the subject of intolerance. He computes that the surface of the earth equals only the two hundred and fortieth part of the superficies of the various globes moving about the sun, and that if every part of the heavens contained only as many suns in proportion, as Dr. Herschell has actually discovered in one part, that our globe would only make the 17,000,000,000 part of the probable planetary surface. 'Shall 'the inhabitants then (says he) of this grain of sand; shall a *few* 'of our number pretend that they alone know the manner in which 'we ought to worship the supreme master of the world? Their 'habitation is a point in the infinity of space; their life only one of 'those innumerable moments that compose eternity; their time 'but the twinkling of an eye in that succession of ages, in which 'generation after generation is lost, and new generations disappear. 'And will they dare announce to present and to future times, 'that divine vengeance cannot be escaped, if we vary in the least 'from the use and practice of their worship? What idea have they 'of the relation established between one God of the universe, and 'the atoms dispersed in the vast empire of nature? Let them raise, 'if they can, with their feeble hands, one of the ends of that veil 'which covers so many mysteries; let them consider a moment, 'the prodigies that roll over their heads; let them attempt to pass 'that awful immensity which their view cannot penetrate, nor their 'imagination surround; and let them determine whether it is by 'their outward appearance, the noise of their instruments, the into-'nation of their chants, or the pomp of their ceremonies, that this 'all-powerful God is to know them, and distinguish their homa-'ges. Is it by the *pride* of our opinions, that we shall think to 'reach the supreme being? Is it not more temperate and reasonable, 'to think that all the people of the earth have access to his throne; 'and that the sovereign master of the universe has permitted us to 'raise ourselves to him by a profound sentiment of love and grati-'tude, the surest tie between man and his creator?—It must be to suppose the mind material, says M. Necker, to say that it can be acted upon by *force*.

ARTICLE XV.

The Speech *of Monf.* Rabaud de Saint Etienne,

A PROTESTANT MINISTER,

In the National Affembly of France, on Thurfday, the twenty-feventh of Auguft, 1789.

The Queftion was,---" *Whether any perfon ought either to be molefted on account of his religious opinions, or debarred from his adherence to that form of worfhip of which he moft approves?*"

I RISE, as the delegate of a numerous and refpectable body of conftituents. The bailiwick which I have the honour to reprefent contains five hundred thoufand inhabitants, amongft whom one hundred and twenty thoufand are proteftants; and in this multitude I have the pleafure to be included. They have inftructed me to afk for an impartial code; and, upon this occafion, I am confident that I can unanfwerably eftablifh the juftice and the propriety of their requeft. The rights which I claim, and in the fupport of which I am now ready to contend, belong equally to you and to ourfelves. They are not merely the rights of the French: They are the rights of all mankind! He who attacks the freedom of his fellow-creatures is only fit to live in flavery! Freedom is a privilege, at once facred and inviolable, which men bring with them into the world, and which is defigned to influence the whole of their opinions. The freedom of thought is paramount to all power whatfoever; and its fanctuary is the heart!— To fetter the confcience is injuftice! to enfnare or to rebel againft it, is an act of facrilege: but, to torture it by the attempt to force its feelings from their propriety, is horrible intolerance; it is the moft abandoned violation of all the maxims of morality and religion! Error, far from being *guilt*, is *truth* in the idea of the perfon by whom it has been embraced. Where is the man who can either prefume to affert that *his* reafoning and confequent procedures are unexceptionable, or venture pofitively to decide againft the fuppofed miftaken fentiments and conduct of his neighbour? A form of worfhip is a tenet: a tenet depends upon opinion: and opinion and liberality are infeparable. To endeavour to compel one perfon to receive a tenet different from that which may have been entertained by another, is a direct attack againft liberty! It is intolerant; and, of courfe, unjuft: it is that kind of perfecution which

which, whilst it insults a manly and independent style of thinking, abets and cherishes hypocrisy!

The last edict which professes to be in favour of those who are not within the pale of the catholic church, grants to them only such indulgences *as it was impossible to have refused*. This is, word for word, the language of the king, who, in his edict, uses these terms: "*I speak of the right of legalising their marriages and their baptisms,* "*and of the permission to bury their dead.*" O humiliating concessions! O degraded Frenchmen! And, is it in *this* enlightened country, and during the eighteenth century, that the nation remains divided into two classes, one of which has long groaned under proscriptions shocking in the extreme? I will speak out at once, and tell this assembly, that the *pretended* gift of the last year was received with shame and concern. We scorn to prove guilty of hypocrisy: at least, we will not degrade ourselves into the objects of your disdain; but, if it be our hard fate still to experience your jealousy and your persecution, we will maintain unsullied the true principle of French honour, one great criterion of which is a contempt for that dissimulation which would debase the intention of the legislature. We do not solicit *favours*: we ask only for *justice*; and, doubtless, that *impartial* liberty which reigns in this assembly will never suffer justice to be dispensed by *partial* distributions. The protestants are, *all*, for their country; and, yet, this country has not granted to *them* any benefits: *they* have no motive to excite emulation; nor are they permitted to enjoy the rewards of either their civil or military virtues. It is not for toleration that I plead. As to *intolerance*, that *savage* word, I hope that it is expunged, for ever, from our annals. Toleration suggests the idea of pity, which degrades the dignity of man; but, liberty ought to be the same in favour of all the world. I demand liberty for those proscribed people; for those wretched wanderers from place to place, over the whole surface of the globe; for those numerous victims to humiliation: I mean the persecuted Jews.

It may, perhaps be answered, that the states which surround you are an exception to those who do not profess the religion of the majority. Natives of France! *you* were made, not to *receive* but, to *afford* examples. And yet if you delight in imitation, copy the Americans!—*They* have excepted no person whatsoever. The follower of that kind of religion which inculcates the true principles of liberty, is intitled to enjoy all the sacred privileges which are attached to human nature.

But I return to my principles, or rather to your own, when I declare that *all men are born and remain free*. Is not *this* the proper consecration of the liberty of the human race? Every exclusive privilege in matters of religion destroys your principles.

principles. *Your* law is only the law which the strongest arm maintains: and, could I not, for the purposes of justifying an act of disobedience, avail myself, against your own authority, of those very principles which have so strongly marked the recent regulation of your conduct?

A long and bloody epoch has made us learn experience. It is not, therefore, full time totally to demolish those abominable barriers which separate man from man; which disunite the French from the French?

My country is *free!* let her discover that she merits this felicity by equally dividing her privileges among all her children! Until the constitution shall have established that equality which I demand, I vote entirely in favour of the proposition of Monsieur de Castellane:—*That no person should be either molested on account of his religious opinions, or debarred from an adherence to that form of worship of which he most approves.*

ARTICLE XVI.

State Measures respecting Dissententers from the National Religion in France.

IF we are to credit the respectable M. de Malsherbes, Lewis the XIVth was cajoled by his clergy into the revocation of the edict of Nantes (which gave toleration to the protestants of France) and was at last led to believe, that the effect of his persecution had been such, that there were no longer any protestants remaining in his kingdom. The courts of law adopted the same presumption by way of a fiction of law; but facts becoming too notorious for them to persist in this, the magistrates endeavoured to soften, or elude the law till at length, in 1787, it was judged prudent to issue an edict, declaring that protestants might enjoy legal marriage and burial, with some other privileges.

But this limited state of toleration was fortunately only the prelude of a more extensive liberty, than is now enjoyed by sectaries in England, or any other European country.

In August 1789, the following articles formed part of the *Declaration of the Rights of Men and Citizens*, made by the National Assembly of France (by whom they are called *sacred*) which have since received the solemn and reiterated sanction of the king of the French: viz.

I. Men

I. Men were born and always continue free, and equal in respect of their rights. Civil diftinctions, therefore, can be founded only on public utility.

II. The end of all political affociations is the prefervation of the natural and imprefcriptible rights of man; and thefe rights are liberty, property, fecurity, and refiftance of oppreffion.

III. Political liberty confifts in the power of doing whatever does not injure another. The exercife of the natural rights of every man, has no other limits than thofe which are neceffary to fecure to every *other* man the free exercife of the fame rights; and thefe limits are determinable only by the law.

IV. The law ought to prohibit only actions hurtful to fociety. What is not prohibited by the law fhould not be hindered; nor fhould any one be compelled to that which the law does not require.

V. The law is an expreffion of the will of the community. All citizens have a right to concur, either perfonally, or by their reprefentatives, in its formation. It fhould be the fame to all, whether it protects or punifhes; and all being equal in its fight, are equally eligible to all honours, places, and employments, according to their different abilities, without any other diftinction than that created by their virtues and talents.

VI. No man ought to be molefted on account of his opinions, not even on account of his *religious* opinions, provided his avowal of them does not difturb the public order eftablifhed by the law.

VII. The unreftrained communication of thoughts and opinions being one of the moft precious rights of man, every citizen may fpeak, write, and publifh freely, provided he is refponfible for the abufe of this liberty in cafes determined by the law.

VIII. A public force being neceffary to give fecurity to the rights of men and of citizens, that force is inftituted for the benefit of the community, and not for the particular benefit of the perfons with whom it is entrufted.

Dec. 24, 1789, in purfuance of thefe generous fentiments, the National Affembly decreed, 1ft. That non-catholics who fhall in other refpects have fulfilled the conditions prefcribed in its preceding decrees, whether as electors, or as perfons eligible, may be chofen without exception into any of the fituations of adminiftration. 2d. That non-catholics are capable of all employments civil and military, equal with other citizens; nothing being hereby decided neverthelefs, refpecting the jews, upon whofe condition the National Affembly referves to itfelf hereafter to pronounce.—Moreover, no motive of exclufion can be oppofed to the eligibility of any citizen, excepting fuch as fhall refult from the decrees made concerning the conftitution.

N. B.

N. B. A fair prospect has since opened in favor of the whole body of the jews in France.

ARTICLE XVII.

An Act for establishing Religious Freedom, passed in the Assembly of Virginia, in the beginning of the Year 1786.

WELL aware, that Almighty God, has created the mind free: that all attempts to influence it by temporal punishments or burthens, or by civil incapacitations, tend only to beget habits of hypocrisy, and are a departure from the plan of the Holy Author of our religion, who being lord of body and mind, yet chose not to propagate it by coercions on either;—that the *impious* presumption of *legislators and rulers, civil and ecclesiastical* (who being themselves but fallible and uninspired men, have assumed dominion over the faith of others, setting up their own opinion and modes of thinking as alone true and infallible, and as such endeavouring to impose them on others), hath established and maintained false religions over the greatest part of the world, and through all time;— that to compel a man to furnish contributions of money for the propagation of opinions which he disbelieves, is sinful and tyrannical;—that even the forcing a man to support this or that teacher of his own religious persuasion, is depriving him of the comfortable liberty of giving his contributions to the particular pastor, whose morals he would make his pattern and whose powers he feels most persuasive to righteousness; and withdrawing from the ministry, those temporal rewards, which proceeding from an approbation of their personal conduct, are an additional incitement to earnest and unremitted labours for the instruction of mankind;—that our civil rights have no dependence on our religious opinions, more than on our opinions in physic or geometry;—that, therefore, the prescribing any citizen as unworthy the public confidence, by laying upon him an incapacity of being called to offices of trust and emolument, unless he profess or renounce this or that religious opinion, is depriving him injuriously of those privileges and advantages to which in common with his fellow-citizens, he has a natural right; and tends also to corrupt the principles of that very religion it is meant to encourage, by bribing with a monopoly of worldly honors and emoluments, those who will externally conform to it;—that though indeed those are criminal who do not withstand such temptations, yet

yet neither are those innocent who lay them in their way;—that to suffer the civil magistrate to intrude his powers into the field of opinion, and to restrain the profession or propagation of principles on a supposition of their ill tendency, is a dangerous fallacy, which at once destroys all religious liberty; because he, being of course judge of that tendency, will make his opinions the rule of judgment, and approve or condemn the sentiments of others, only as they shall agree with or differ from his own; that it is time enough for the rightful purposes of civil government, for its officers to interpose, when principles break out in overt acts against peace and good order;—and finally, that truth is great, and will prevail if left to herself; is the proper and sufficient antagonist to error; and can have nothing to fear from the conflict, unless (by human interposition) disarmed of her natural weapons, free argument and debate; errors ceasing to be dangerous, when it is permitted freely to contradict them:

"Be it therefore enacted by the general assembly, that no man shall be compelled to support any religious worship, place, or ministry whatsoever; nor shall be forced, restrained, molested or burthened in his body or goods, nor shall otherwise suffer, on account of his religious opinions or belief: but all men be free to profess, and by argument to maintain, their opinion in matters of religion; and that the same shall in no wise diminish, enlarge, or affect their civil capacities.

"And though we well know that this assembly, elected by the people for the ordinary purposes of legislation only, have no power to restrain the acts of succeeding assemblies, constituted with powers equal to our own; and that therefore, to declare this act irrevocable, would be of no effect in law; yet we are free to declare, and do declare, that the rights hereby asserted, are natural rights of mankind; and that if any act shall be hereafter passed to repeal the present, or to narrow its operation, such act will be no infringement of natural rights."

ARTICLE XVIII.

A Parable against Persecution, by Dr. Franklin, in Imitation of Scripture Language; founded upon a Jewish Tradition *.

AND it came to pass after these things, that Abraham sat in the door of his tent, about the going down of the sun. And behold a man bent with age, coming from the way of the wilderness leaning

---

* ' The following parable against persecution was communicated to me,' says Lord ' Kairns, ' by Doctor Franklin, of Philadelphia, a man who makes a great figure in the ' lienated

leaning on a staff. And Abraham arose and met him, and said unto him, turn in I pray thee and wash thy feet, and tarry all night; and thou shalt arise early in the morning, and go on thy way. And the man said, nay; for I will abide under this tree. But Abraham pressed him greatly: so he turned and they went into the tent: and Abraham baked unleavened bread, and they did eat. And when Abraham saw that the man blessed not God, he said unto him, wherefore dost thou not worship the most high God, creator of heaven and earth? And the man answered and said, I do not worship thy God, neither do I call upon his name; for I have made to myself a God, which abideth always in my house, and provideth me with all things. And Abraham's zeal was kindled against the man, and he arose, and fell upon him, and drove him forth with blows into the wilderness. And God called unto Abraham, saying, Abraham, where is the stranger? And Abraham answered and said, Lord, he would not worship thee, neither would he call upon thy name; therefore have I driven him out from before my face into the wilderness. And God said, have I borne with him these hundred and ninety and eight years, and nourished him and clothed him, notwithstanding his rebellion against me; and couldst not thou who art thyself a sinner, bear with him one night?

Extracts from Observations on the Peopling of Countries, &c. By the same.

THE great increase of offspring in particular families is not always owing to greater fecundity of nature, but sometimes to examples of industry in the heads, and industrious education; by which the children are enabled to provide better for themselves, and their marrying early is encouraged from the prospect of good subsistence. If there be a sect therefore, in our nation, that regard frugality and industry as religious duties, and educate their children therein, more than others commonly do; such sect must consequently increase more by natural generation, than any other sect in Britain *.

‘ learned world; and who would still make a greater figure for benevolence and candour, were virtue as much regarded in this declining age as knowledge.
‘ The historical style of the Old Testament is here finely imitated; and the moral must strike every one who is not sunk in stupidity and superstition. Were it really a chapter of Genesis, one is apt to think, that persecution could never have shown a bare face among the Jews or Christians. But, alas! that is a vain thought. Such a passage in the Old Testament, would avail as little against the rancorous passions of men, as the following passages in the New Testament, though persecution cannot be condemned in terms more explicit. " He that is weak in the faith receive you, but not to doubtful disputations. For, &c."
* See another letter by Dr. Franklin on the subject of religious liberty, in this collection, page 66.

ARTICLE XIX.

Extract from the Address of the Religious Society called Quakers, from their yearly Meeting for Pensylvania, New-Jersey, Delaware, and the Western Parts of Maryland and Virginia, to the President of the United State, Oct. 1789.

The free toleration which the citizens of these states enjoy in the public worship of the Almighty, agreeable to the dictates of their consciences, we esteem among the choicest of blessings;—and as we desire to be filled with fervent charity for those who differ from us in faith and practice, believing that the general assembly of saints is composed of the sincere and upright hearted of all nations, kingdoms, and people, so we trust we may justly claim it from others: and in a full persuasion, that the divine principles we profess, leads unto harmony and concord, we can take no part in carrying on war, on any occasion or under any power, but are bound in conscience to lead quiet and peaceable lives, in godliness and honesty, amongst men, contributing freely our proportion to the indigencies of the poor, and to the necessary support of civil government, acknowledging those who rule well to be worthy of double honour; and if any, professing with us, are or have been of a contrary disposition or conduct, we own them not therein; having never been chargeable, from our first establishment as a religious society, with fomenting or countenancing tumults or conspiracies, or disrespect to those who are put in authority over us.

The Answer of the President of the United States, to the Address of the Religious Society called Quakers, &c.

GENTLEMEN,

I RECEIVED with pleasure your affectionate Address, and thank you for the friendly sentiments and good wishes which you express for the success of my administration, and for my present happiness.

We have reason to rejoice in the prospect, that the present national government, which by the favour of Divine Providence, was formed by the common counsels, and peaceably established with the common consent of the people, will prove a blessing to every denomination of them.—To render it such, my best endeavours shall not be wanting.

Government being among other purposes instituted to protect the persons and consciences of men from oppression, it certainly is the

only

only duty of rulers not only to abstain from it themselves, but according to their stations to prevent it in others.

The liberty enjoyed by the people of these States of worshipping Almighty God agreeably to their consciences, is not only among the choicest of their *blessings*, but also of their *rights*. While men perform their social duties faithfully, they do all that society or the State can with propriety demand or expect, and remain responsible only to their Maker for the religion or modes of faith which they may prefer or profess. Your principles and conduct are well known to me, and it is doing the people called Quakers no more than justice to say, that (except their declining to share with others the burthen of the common defence) there is no denomination among us who are more exemplary and useful citizens.

I assure you very explicitly, that, in my opinion, the conscientious scruples of all men should be treated with great delicacy and tenderness; and it is my wish and desire, that the laws may always be as extensively accommodated to them, as a due regard to the protection and essential interests of the nation, may justify and permit.

GEORGE WASHINGTON.

Extract from an Address of the Convention of the Protestant Episcopal Church, in the States of New York, New Jersey, Pensylvania, Delaware, Maryland, Virginia, and South Carolina, at Philadelphia, 7th August, 1789, to General Washington, *President of the United States of America.*

PERMIT us to add, that as the representatives of a numerous and extended church, we most thankfully rejoice in the election † of a civil ruler deservedly beloved, and eminently distinguished among the friends of genuine religion—who has happily united a tender regard for other churches with an inviolable attachment to his own.

Extract from General Washington's *Answer.*

THE consideration that human happiness and moral duty are inseparably connected, will always continue to prompt me to promote the progress of the former, by inculcating the practice of the latter.—On this occasion it will ill become me to conceal the joy I have felt in perceiving the fraternal affection which appears to en-

---

† They say it is the first instance known of a governor appointed by unanimous consent.—General Washington it is to be observed is a member of the Episcopal Church, and a great observer of attendance upon public worship of Sundays.

crease

crease every day among the friends of genuine religion. It affords edifying prospects indeed, to see christians of different denominations dwell together in more charity and conduct themselves in respect to each other with a more christian like spirit, than ever they have done in any former age, or in any other nation.

ARTICLE XX.

Facts and Observations respecting the situation of the Jews in England.

IT is difficult to ascertain at what time the Jews first settled in England, but there seem to have been considerable numbers of them established here before the conquest.*—Those numbers were much encreased by William the Conqueror, who, for a stipulated sum of money, brought hither a pretty large colony of Jews from Rouen, in Normandy.—Under his successors, down to the time of Edward the 1st, there were so many of that religion resident in England, that particular ordinances were made for their government, a peculiar court of justice was appropriated, and a judge appointed for the determination of their suits; and they were allowed to have a Jury *de medietate*:† But neither their numbers, nor their riches (which appear to have been very considerable) gained them any respect. On the contrary, they were treated with the utmost contempt and cruelty, by all orders of men. They were distinguished by a peculiar dress,§ looked on as the meanest vassals, as the absolute property of the crown, and as an order of beings so much inferior to the human species, that to contract marriage with them was classed among the most infamous crimes, and punished with death.‖

The monarchs of those times, whose tyranny over their other subjects often met with very formidable opposition from the great Barons

---

* See the Archæologia, vol. 8. p. 389.   † Prynne's Dem. pt. 2. p. 105.
§ Stat. de *Judaismo*, sect. 4. 2. Spelm. Concil. 188, 387. Prynne's Dem. 2 pt. p. 18. 101.
‖ *Contrahentes cum Judæis vel Judæabus, pecorantes, & Sodomitæ in terra vivi confodiantur*—Fleta, Lib. 1. c. 37.—By a council held at Worcester, in 1240, it was forbidden all Christian women to give suck to any Jewish child. *Prohibemus etiam sub interminatione anathematis, ne mulieres Christianæ pueros nutriant Judæorum.* By the council of Exeter, held in 1287, Christians were forbidden to eat with Jews, or even to accept medicines from them when sick. 2 Spelm. *Concil,* 256, 386.

What

Barons, and from haughty churchmen, found in the Jews a people over whom they might exercise their pride, their rapaciousness, and their cruelty, without resistance or control. It is true, that these crimes of the Norman Kings were disguised under the name of punishments for very great enormities imputed to the Jews; such as the frequent crucifying of children at Easter, in derision of Jesus Christ; but these enormities, it has been well observed, were never heard of but at times when the king's coffers required to be replenished ‡

The tyranny indeed of the crown, when exercised over this unhappy race, far from being resisted, seems even to have been popular; and, upon some occasions, the people who were nearly in a state of slavery themselves, took upon them to play the tyrants, and to persecute the Jews† with unrelenting barbarity. A very memorable instance of this kind happened at the coronation of Richard 1st, when the populace of London and of several other cities, plundered and massacred, in cold blood, every Jew who fell into their hands; and that for no other crime, than because some few of that religion had dared, with their profane eyes, to sully so holy a spectacle.

All the other outrages which were offered to this devoted race are, as well as this, to be imputed, in a great degree, to the superstition of those times, predominant alike over the princes and the

---

What is mentioned by Fleta seems to have been the law in most of the countries in Europe. Even so late as in the reign of Philip 2d, we find in the work of a celebrated Flemish lawyer, Josse de Damhoudere, which is entitled *Pratique Judiciare et causes criminelles* and was printed at Antwerp in 1564, the following passage: It is in the chapter *Du vilain et enorme peche contre Nature.*

Il y a encores une autre espece, laquelle semble avoir participation & affinite avec les susdictes especes: Car elle n'est denaturelle, mais toutefois à la consideration & regard de notre foy, est pour telle tenue & reputée, & les malfaicteurs punis comme sodomites; asçavoir ceux, qui ont à faire avec Turcs, Sarrasins, ou Juifz: Car iceux les droicts & notre saincte foy ne les tiennent pour autres que bestes; non pas par nature, mais pour leur tres dure malice.

‡ Another crime of which the Jews were accused, was the circumcising of Christian children.—Mr. Selden has cited a record of one of these convictions, which was made upon the testimony of a great number of witnesses, as well laymen as priests, that the part, supposed to have been circumcised, was swoln. Afterwards, upon the requisition of the Jews, the child was inspected, when he appeared to be uncircumcised; but this, says Mr. Selden, was not repugnant to the former testimony, seeing, by surgery, the skin may be drawn forth to an uncircumcision; and for this he cites some authorities.—Selden's Works, vol. 3. p. 1461.

† Several towns procured it to be granted to them in their charters, that no Jew should from thenceforth reside or remain within their walls.—Molloy *de jure marit.* p. 471. Prynne's Dem. pt. 2. p. 23. 25.

people, who seem to have considered the persecution and oppression of the Jews as a kind of religious crusade,‡ and a service most acceptable to God. ¶—It is only by such motives as these, that it is possible to account for the conduct of Edward the 1st, who in the year 1290 put the last hand to the persecution of this people, and banished them all out of his dominions, on pain of death if they returned§; because it was a measure which a much weaker prince than Edward must have seen was manifestly contrary to his interest; since this people, to say nothing of the increase of population and of opulence, which they brought into the country, had at all times afforded a constant supply of treasure to the avarice, and of victims to the cruelty of himself and his predecessors.*

In this state of exile the Jews continued for three centuries and a half, without any attempt being made to recall them. But when the English government was changed to a republic, Holland became in many respects an object of emulation to England, and the advantages which had resulted to that country, from a toleration of the Jews, did not escape observation. The detestation too of papism, which at that time prevailed or rather raged in England, had inspired many persons with favorable dispositions towards the Jews. Several motions were made in parliament in their favor,** and though none of them met with success, yet they afforded encouragement to the Jews of Amsterdam, to make some overtures for an establishment in England. A negociation for that purpose was determined

‡ In the year 1189, a great number of Jews were murdered, and their houses pillaged by the pilgrims and other persons who had taken the cross, and were about to set out for Jerusalem.—Prynne's Dem. pt. 1. p. 11. One of the men who had thus greatly enriched himself by the plunder of the Jews, was afterwards himself robbed and murdered by his host, who was likewise a Christian: The populace however considered him as a saint and a martyr. ib. 13.

¶ It is not a century ago since the council of Jamaica petitioned King William to banish the Jews from that island, because they were "the descendants of the crucifiers of the blessed Jesus." Hist. of Jamaica, vol. 2. p. 293.

§ The number of Jews thus banished was, according to Sir Edward Coke, (2 Inst. 508.) 15,060; according to Mat. Westm. (Flores hist. an. 1290) 16,511.

* This expulsion of the Jews was so acceptable to the nation, that the parliament, by way of recompence, immediately voted the king a 15th.—Prynne indeed, insists in his Demurrer, that the banishment of the Jews was not an act of the king's, but a legislative act, done with the consent of parliament. The English nation seems to have the disgrace of having first set the example of this cruel treatment of the Jews; an example which was afterwards followed in most countries in Europe: for the Jews were all banished out of France by Philip the Fair, in the year 1307; out of Castille by John 2, in 1430; out of the rest of Spain by Ferdinand, in 1492; out of Portugal, by Emanuel, in 1497; out of Germany, in 1385; and out of Sicily and Naples in 1539, by Charles 5th.

** Thurloe's State Papers, vol. I. p. 387.

on, and Menaſſeh Ben Iſrael was choſen to conduct it. That venerable Rabbi § accordingly came into England; and prevailed ſo far with Cromwell, that the Protector took the Propoſals which he made on behalf of his brethren into ſerious conſideration. — That he might proceed with more caution, Cromwell ſummoned to his council two of the judges, ſeven citizens, and fourteen clergymen for their advice; and the queſtions he propoſed to them were, whether it were lawful to re-admit the Jews into England; and if it were, upon what terms they ſhould be admitted. But after four days had been ſpent in diſputation among the miniſters, Cromwell diſmiſſed them without coming to any determination, and aſſured them that they had left him much more uncertain than they found him.

The project of recalling the Jews ſeems at this period to have been very unpopular with the lower ranks of the people, ‡ and even with ſome perſons of education and learning. Among theſe, the perſon moſt active in his oppoſition to the Jews, was William Prynne; a barriſter, then already diſtinguiſhed for the learning and ſtill more for the boldneſs of his publications in the reign of Charles I. and during the common-wealth, and for the extraordinary ſeverities which he had ſuffered, under both thoſe governments. In order to prevent the ſucceſs of the application made by the Jews, or to uſe his own words, that he might raiſe "a perpetual bar to " the anti-chriſtian Jews' re-admiſſion into England, both in that " new-fangled age and all future generation;" ‖ he publiſhed a work in two parts, which he entitled " a ſhort demurrer to the " Jews long diſcontinued barred remitter into England." This work, which ſeems to have been intended not only to diſpoſe the nation to refuſe admittance to the Jews, but likewiſe to terrify the Jews themſelves and diſguſt them with the project, contains a very faithful narrative of the pretended crimes and real ſufferings of the Jews under the Norman Kings, till the time of their baniſhment. That baniſhment the Author inſiſts was by act of parliament, and therefore he contends that it was by parliament alone that they could be recalled. * That the recall of the Jews would be impious, he ſeeks to prove by many texts of ſcripture; by the following among

§ See Dict. de Moreri. art. Menaſſeh Ben Iſrael.
† See a narrative of this tranſaction printed at the time, and referred to in Tovey's Anglia Judaica, p. 268. See too Thurloe's State Papers, vol. IV. p. 321.
‡ Prynne tells us, that as he walked along the ſtreets, he heard the beggars and poor people complaining that they muſt all turn Jews, and that there would be nothing left for the poor. Dem. pt. 1. Addreſs to the reader, p. 4. See too Dem. pt. 1, p. 72, 102.
‖ Dem. pt. 2. Addreſs to the reader, and pt. 1 p. 126.
* Dem. pt. 1, p. 65, 72.

others

others "Salt is good, but if the salt have lost its favor, wherewith
"shall it be seasoned?"§ "it is neither fit for the land nor yet for
"the dunghill, but to be cast out and trodden under foot of men" †
"This" he adds ‡ "is the condition of the Jews, who have lost
"both their Saviour and their favor too: Therefore not fit for our
"land, nor yet for our dunghills, but to be cast out from among us,
"and trodden under foot of all christian men, while unbelievers."
That it would be impolitic, he contends; because the nation was
"already *overstored* with native Englishmen,"‖ and because the Jews
were aliens and foreigners, and foreigners ought not to be received in England from whence they had been frequently banished
"by our ancestors as the greatest pests, inconveniencies, and
"grievances to the natives.* Nature he says will not that sheep
"should be associated with wolves, neither will prudence, that
"natives should be coupled with foreigners; as locusts are to the
"corn, so are foreigners to the republic; they devour the fruit
"of the commonwealth." § He insists, that in such an apostatizing
age, it was to be feared the Jews would make many converts; †
and that Jesuits and popish priests would probably come into England under the disguise of Jews. § To the argument, that admit
ting the Jews into England would be the means of their conversion
to christianity, he answers, that "God can convert them in any
"other country as well as in England,"** and that such individuals
of that religion as really wanted to be converted to christianity, might
be safely admitted, but the rest ought to be excluded.* The argument that they would bring wealth to the state, he despises as
worldly, carnal and sensual; and he asks whether the English ought,
like Judas, to betray and sell their Saviour Christ to the Jews for
thirty pieces of silver; § and he denies that the Jews would enrich
any but themselves. He says, that the Jews "have little reason
'to desire to replant themselves in England, where their ancestors,
"in times past sustained so many miseries, massacres, affronts, op-
"pressions and fleecings upon all occasions, and themselves can
"expect little better usage for the future;" † and, after having mentioned the arbitrary and exorbitant taxes which were formerly im-

§ Matt. V. 13.
† Luke XIV. 34, 35. ‡ Dem. pt. 1, p. 72.
† Dem. pt 1, 82, 93. * Ibid, 97, 98.
§ These are not Prynne's own words, but he cites them with apparent
approbation from the Sphæra Civitatis of Dr. J. Case.
‖ Dem. pt. 1, p. 89. § Ibid.
** Dem. pt. 1, p. 110. * Ibid, 114. § Ibid, 120.
† Ibid, 66.

posed

posed on them, he asks, "are not their taxes, in case they will now "return, likely to be more high, frequent, and oppressive?" ‡

What was the effect of this publication, and what the final result of Cromwell's deliberations, does not appear. Some writers indeed positively assert, that he did give the Jews permission to settle here; ‖ but others * contend, that this permission was not given till after the restoration of Charles II. in the year 1664 or 1665.

From the time when the Jews under this permission re-established themselves in England, they have always been as to all civil rights, exactly in the same situation as christian protestants. Those who were aliens, subject to no more restrictions or disabilities than were imposed on other aliens, and those born in England entitled to all the rights of natural born subjects.

It may seem perhaps presumptuous, to state so positively what the law is, upon a subject, on which Mr. Justice Blackstone § has studiously avoided giving any opinion; but the time when that learned Judge wrote, and much more the ejaculation with which he closes his account of the naturalization act †, give reason to suppose, that his reserve upon this occasion proceeded from timidity, and an unwillingness to revive a controversy which had been carried on with great intemperance; rather than from any doubt which he entertained upon the subject. It has been pretended indeed, that Jews are incapable of holding lands; and in support of that assertion has been cited an act of parliament, said to have passed in the 54th year of the reign of Henry III. and printed by Dr. Tovey in his Anglia Judaica from an ancient manuscript in the Bodleian library. But this act does not exist among the parliament rolls, has never been printed among the statutes, is not mentioned by any of our law writers either ancient or modern, and does not appear to have been ever recognized by any of our courts of justice *. With respect to their *religious* rights, there may be more doubt, for though they do in fact enjoy perfect toleration, yet it is a toleration for which the law seems to afford them no security, the benefits of the Toleration Act † being expressly confined to such only as do

---

‡ Dem. pt. 2, p. 131; and in another place (pt. 2, p. 76) he says; "if the "wealthy Jews in foreign parts have a desire to be impoverished and fleeced "of all their wealth, by incessant arbitrary annual taxes imposed on them, "at the assessor's pleasure, let them now come into England."

‖ Among others, Burnet in the history of his own times.

* Particularly Tovey in his Anglia Judaica.

§ 1 Bl. Com. 375. † "Peace be now to its manes."

* The Jews did in fact before their banishment possess real estates. This appears by Edw. I. immediately after their banishment, seizing upon all their houses and lands, as if escheated to him, and granting them out to different subjects. Prynne's Dem. part. ii, p. 117.

† 1 W. and M. stat. 1. c. 18.

(98)

not deny the Trinity; and in the year 1743, Lord Hardwicke, the then Lord Chancellor, decided that a legacy of a sum of money to found an institution for reading the Jewish law, was illegal and void, as being for the propagation of a religious belief contrary to christianity, which is part of the law and constitution of the kingdom ‡.

Foreign Jews too labour under this disadvantage, that though the stat. of the 13 Geo. c. 7, has enabled them to become natural subjects by a residence of seven years in the American colonies, yet they cannot be naturalized by any other means, because the stat. of 7 Jac. 1. c. 2, enacts, that no person shall be naturalized, who has not received the Sacrament within a month previous to his naturalization. To remove this test in favour of the jews, towards whom it operated as an absolute disability, and to enable them to prefer bills to parliament for their naturalization in common with other foreigners, an act of parliament was passed in the year 1753. The circumstances which gave rise to it were these.

A bill had been brought into parliament in the year 1751, to declare, that all foreign protestants should become naturalized by residence for a certain time in the British dominions. It had been at first proposed, that this bill should extend to jews, as well as protestants; but as it was found that the bill was likely to meet with great opposition, that part of it was abandoned, and it was confined to protestants. The very circumstance, however, by which it had been sought to render the bill more palatable to some persons, made it much less so to others; and it was said, that the only useful part of the measure was that which had been given up, for the only protestants who would come here would be the poor and idle; whereas we might expect many rich jews to establish themselves amongst us, if we gave them protection and encouragement. The bill was finally rejected, but this ground of opposition to it was not forgotten.

That such topics had been advanced without contradiction, seemed to indicate the public opinion upon the subject; and those, who foresaw the great national advantages which must attend the naturalization of foreign jews, would not suffer this, which seemed to be so favourable an opportunity of effecting it, to pass unimproved. The measure however was not hastily pursued, for the bill to carry it into execution was not brought into parliament till March 1753. The caution with which the bill was framed, was remarkable; it was confined to the mere purpose of enabling jews to be naturalized by parliament, and every possible and even every imaginary danger which the most timid mind could suggest, was guarded against with care.

‡ 2 Vezey's Rep. 274.

That

That no unknown or improper persons might be candidates for these advantages, it was provided that no jew should be naturalized, who had not been previously resident three years in Great-Britain or Ireland. That they might have no influence on the established religion, it was declared that they should be incapable of holding any ecclesiastical patronage, or the right of presentation to any church: and that roman catholics might not become natural subjects under the disguise of jews, none were to be naturalized, who could not bring proof of their having professed the jewish religion during the three last preceeding years. Yet even all these anxious precautions did not secure the bill an unanimous approbation, for though it passed without debate through the House of Lords where it originated, yet in the House of Commons it met with very violent opposition, in which (such is the fallibility of human nature) the wise and virtuous Sir John Barnard took the lead. An opposition still more formidable soon discovered itself out of the house*, and many petitions against the bill were presented to the Commons. Amongst these, the most remarkable was a petition from the City of London, in its corporate capacity, which in terms the most vague, but the most emphatic, complained that the "bill tended " greatly to the dishonor of the christian religion, endangered our " excellent constitution, and was highly prejudicial to the interest " and trade of the kingdom in general, and of the City of London " in particular." But notwithstanding these senseless complaints and these marks of public disapprobation, the bill passed the House of Commons by a very large majority, and received the royal assent.

The enemies however to the measure, far from being discouraged by the defeat which they had suffered, only became more violent in their opposition. The question was now discussed in pamphlets in which not only the effects but even the operation of the act, became a subject of dispute; and almost every topic of trade, of policy, and of religion that could be introduced into the controversy was exhausted, on one side or other.

The opposers of the act contended, that it would effect a most alarming change in the condition of the jews; because it would enable them to purchase lands, which the policy of the law had never till then permitted. That it must prove highly injurious to the trading part of the nation, because many of the jews whom it would seduce to settle in this country, would engage in commerce,

---

* It was observed at the time that much of this opposition might have been prevented, if a different title had been given to the bill; and if instead of being called " An act to permit persons professing the Jewish religion to be naturalized," it had been entitled, " An act to prevent jews from profaning the Sacrament of the Lord's Supper."

in which they could not succeed but by the ruin of other merchants, of those who had long ago embarked their fortunes in trade, and who had at great risque and with infinite pains opened new sources of riches to the nation; services, which an ungrateful public was now preparing to recompense by sacrificing them to a troop of foreigners and infidels: that it must likewise occasion a considerable loss to the state by a diminution of the alien's duty. That it might, it was true, allure some persons of opulence to settle in England, but when it was considered what a poor and miserable people the jews in general were, there could be no doubt that it would at the same time deluge the kingdom with an innumerable swarm of vagrants and paupers, who would become an insupportable evil to the country already over-burthened with its poor. That the jews were a fraudulent, an avaricious, and a corrupted nation, ever intent upon their own immediate profit, and strangers to all patriotism and public spirit. That to incorporate such a people amongst us, would be to corrupt our national character for ever, and to engraft upon it vices which could never be repressed. And why, it was asked, are all these evils to be brought upon the nation? Is it to satisfy any moral or any religious duty? Nay, on the contrary, it is to violate all duties of religion, to encourage its most inveterate enemies, and to foster the bitterest revilers of Jesus Christ; it is impiously to resist the will of God, and to attempt to lighten the heaviness of his judgments, since he has declared by the mouths of his prophets, that the jews should be a wretched and a wandering people. Why then in contempt of these prophecies, in contempt of their completion which has already taken place, is this officious and unprofitable zeal discovered in favor of the jews, unless it be with a design of involving this nation in the calamities which yet await that devoted people?

On the other hand it was said, that it was astonishing so much clamor should be excited by an act, which had made so very slight an alteration in our law. That the act established no new principle and effected no innovation, and that it only extended the operation of laws which experience had proved to be highly beneficial to the country. That this was true in whatever character the objects of the bill were considered, whether as Jews or as foreigners; if as Jews, the people of that religion has long been suffered to reside amongst us; if as foreigners, foreigners might be naturalized in England ever since the statute of king James the First. That Jews born in England were capable of holding lands before the passing of the act; or if they were not, the act gave them no such capacity. That it was true, the act would as had been represented, bring many foreigners into the kingdom, and of those foreigners many would engage in commerce; but it was surely the
first

first time that ever it had been pretended, that it was a misfortune to a country to have its inhabitants, its trade, its industry and its riches increased. That it was absurd to suppose, that no new adventurers in commerce could prosper, but at the expence of the old; as if the trade of the country had reached the utmost limit to which it could possibly be carried. That to permit Jews to be naturalized, could only bring into the country the opulent, since it conferred advantages on none but those who had wealth to lay out in land, or to improve in commerce. That if the poor and the indigent of that people were disposed to come amongst us, there was nothing in the law as it before stood, to prevent them. That the fact however was, that none of the jewish poor were or could be a burthen to the nation, because they were always supported by the rich of their own religion. That as to the character of the Jews, their religious doctrines inculcated no immoralities, so that if they had all the vices which were laid to their charge, it could be imputed to nothing but the restraints, the severities and the persecution to which they had been exposed; and, that cause being removed, the effect would cease with it. That as to their pretended want of patriotism and public spirit, recent facts had clearly disproved it, since in the late rebellion some of the Jewish religion were the most forward to exert themselves in the defence of the established government, at the risque both of their property and their lives. That in the last place, the measure was represented as impious, as hostile to religion, destructive of the judgments of God and repugnant to his prophecies; as if there could be any impiety in opening an asylum to those who were distressed, as if persecution were a duty of religion, as if the judgments of God could be counteracted by man, or his prophecies required the aid of human concurrence to be fulfilled. That the calamities which awaited this country if they protected the jews, were those only which had befallen Venice, Leghorn, Amsterdam, and every other country which had afforded them protection; an increase of trade, population, riches, and every kind of prosperity.

Such were the arguments which were used on either side of this controversy; but arguments were not to decide it. A clamor was raised throughout the kingdom: a general election was approaching: and the minister, Mr. Pelham, had not courage enough to encounter the popular odium at such a juncture. It was determined therefore, that the act should be repealed.

At the ensuing sessions, there appeared in the parliament an eagerness for the repeal, which could hardly have been surpassed, if the fate of the empire had depended on it. All parties were impatient to shew their zeal in so good a cause, and the zeal of some members was quickened by instructions and addresses from their constituents. Among the foremost in voting these addresses, were the freeholders of *Warwickshire*.

On the very first day of the sessions, and in both houses of parliament, at the same time, a motion was made for leave to bring in a bill to repeal this obnoxious act. In the house of Lords, the Duke of Newcastle himself made the motion; and in the House of Commons, it was made by Sir James Dashwood, one of the leaders of opposition; and seconded by Lord Parker who was attached to the ministry. The bill for the repeal met indeed with some opposition in both Houses, particularly from Lord Temple in the House of Peers; but all opposition was ineffectual; the bill for the repeal was carried through both Houses by very large majorities, and was the very first act passed in the session; and that the disgrace of the nation might be perpetuated, the act recites as the cause of the repeal, " that occasion had been taken from the " said act to raise discontents, and to disquiet the minds of his " Majesty's subjects*.

The Duke of Newcastle indeed thought, that even the passing this act was not sufficient to expiate the crime which he had committed in the eyes of the vulgar. Not satisfied therefore with moving for a repeal of every part of the act which could be beneficial to the Jews, he proposed to leave that clause which disabled all Jews from purchasing or inheriting advowsons, or presentations to any ecclesiastical benefice, still in force. This however was strenuously and successfully opposed, because the suffering that solitary clause to remain unrepealed, might seem it was thought, to countenance by implication the dangerous doctrine which had been lately maintained, that Jews were capable of possessing real estates.

This wretched attempt to serve the Jews seemed indeed to have opened the eyes of some part of the nation to dangers, of which before they never had been conscious; and to have convinced them that it was the part of good citizens not to extend, but to contract their indulgence to the Jews. No sooner therefore had the repeal passed, then Lord Harley moved for leave to bring in a bill to repeal so much of the act of the 13th of George the 2d. as related to Jews who should come to settle in any British colony after a certain time. It was not possible however to persuade the House, that there was much mischief to be dreaded from a law which had produced no one bad effect during the 14 years of its existence, and under which the colonies had become every day more flourishing, and the motion was rejected.

* 27 Geo. II. c. 1.

ARTICLE

ARTICLE XXI.

I. *Letter of a Christian Politician.*

IT is a persuasion with some that the Protestant Dissenters are in general turbulent and seditious; and it is a natural persuasion, inasmuch as it is founded upon ancient prejudices; but it is certainly destitute of modern proofs; and were it true, it is evidently pursued into false consequences, for civil laws being limited to civil objects, it is under this description alone, and not under a religious one, that men are subject to the civil power. Nothing indeed is more natural than that persons long deprived of some of the best privileges of citizens, on account of their being sectaries, should be ready and adroit in arguing both for civil and religious liberty; or that men who have been saved by means of a revolution from civil despotism and the horrors which formerly attended Popery, should adhere to revolution principles. There seems no mischief in the people being sometimes reminded of their natural rights, when it is so generally the endeavour of persons in power to make them forget them; and as to revolution principles, they were once courtly principles, while they were thought necessary to secure a throne, but they are now it seems reprobated by courtiers, when they can only be useful to the public. If the clergy are offended with the propagation of principles of civil and religious liberty, or with any spirited conduct in the Dissenters, they must take the blame upon themselves; for if they had not supported laws, imposing the disabilities by which the Dissenters are checked in the profession and practice of their religion, the Dissenters naturally would have differed very little in political matters from the members of the establishment. But after admitting that there are many active partizans among the Dissenters, which some may be inclined to think is one of their merits, I apprehend that the majority of them will be found to have been disposed to a quiet and accommodating conduct; owing, in general, to their easy circumstances, their love of the House of Brunswick, and the sober morals in which they are usually educated. Had their numbers approached nearer to those of the established church, they might have been fond of the pursuit of power whenever accompanied with a hope of obtaining it; but their weakness has long made them contented with taking a defensive part; and the progress of liberal principles has now set their prospects of superiority so wholly out of sight, that if they had even the *injustice,* as well as *folly,* to entertain such extravagancies, the nation, in these times, would never tolerate any new set of

candidates

candidates for religious tyranny, and particularly one, which they have held in a sort of hereditary contempt and aversion.

Instead of censuring the Dissenters for using too bold a language in their lately published resolutions on the subject of the Test Laws, I think they have fallen short of what the case admitted and required, thereby furnishing a proof of the difficulty of reconciling the majority of the Dissenters to any other than moderate measures. I cannot say how long this diffidence will last, for men in the right, when once they are assembled together, naturally acquire courage and extent of views, and supported as they are by foreign examples, and by the express or tacit authority of the most eminent modern writers of every nation, an opposition to them will only serve to make them more combined as well as more determined. For my own part, I wish they had used a still more decided tone; and had I possessed any influence over their meetings, I should have advised a publication like the following, composed of a statement of facts and resolutions.

FACTS.

The Protestant Dissenters pay, without hesitation, all taxes to the church, as well as to the state, equally with the Members of the establishment; and they have both served and saved each of them in times of difficulty and danger. They are nevertheless, on account of their religious principles, declared incapable of holding offices (civil or military,) of serving in corporations, of being rewarded by the public, or of exercising various professions or trusts, unless they receive within a certain term, the sacrament of the Lord's supper, administered according to the particular rites of the church of England, as a proof of their fitness or qualification. If they decline this *test*, the penalty on their appearing in any of these situations, is not only avoidance of the office, &c. but the party is disabled from suing, either in law or equity; from being the guardian of any child, or the executor or administrator of any person, or from receiving any legacy or deed of gift, or bearing any office, and forfeits besides 500l. These penalties, from neglect or accident, would often fall upon persons of the church of England, were not acts of indemnity passed from time to time, to suspend their operation. But the repeal of the law itself is denied, and some corporation officers are now actually prosecuted under it.

Upon these facts are founded the following

RESOLUTIONS.

That it is the right of every man, where it can be done without violating any civil duties, not only to express his thoughts; but openly to act according to them.

That

That this is especially true in the concerns of men with their universal creator, wantonly to interfere in which, is to violate rights both human and divine.

That no one has ever proved, that the Dissenters, considered as dissenters, are in the habit of violating or neglecting any civil duties.

That where they offend individually only, the law should operate individually only, with them, as with other citizens; and not oppress all of them constantly for the possible occasional offences of a few.

That no society is to be ruled arbitrarily, even by its majority; but the majority is to seek the interest of the *whole*, wherever the whole can share, and not that of the majority solely; and if laws are enforced upon a different principle, it is not force which can render laws just.

That when the dissenting minority in religious concerns, besides supporting their own clergy, contribute to pay the clergy of the majority, they perform a double duty; and are not therefore to be excluded from *civil* stations, to which they equally contribute, and to which their religious tenets have plainly no unfavourable relation, as sectaries in general possess at least morality.

That men who are unnecessarily excluded from serving their country, or benefiting themselves in public stations, are really injured by having that *withheld* from them, which should naturally be free to all; for wrongs, it is evident, may be *negative* at well as positive.

That civil government was instituted to prevent persecution, and not to enforce it, and least of all in the case of religion, which merely *as such* is not cognizable by man.

That those sects which insist upon an explicit acknowledgment of their legal capacity to serve the public, are not therefore to be accused of an undue love of power or profit; but rather will that sect be chargeable with it, which shall seek to monopolize every thing.

That when the Dissenters are declared by law unfit to serve their king and country, a stigma is fixed upon their characters, which it would be the greatest of stigmas if they were not anxious to remove.

That it is an insult to the legislature to suppose, that it must not or will not do justice in the present question, because it may be at a loss where to stop upon other occasions.

That it is a still greater insult to common sense to suppose, that dissenters who may sit in either House of Parliament, cannot be trusted in executing laws which they have been trusted in making.

That the power which says it can tolerate at pleasure, implies that it can persecute at pleasure; and hence the Dissenters do not ask for toleration as a favour, but for liberty as a right.

That the Dissenters plead more than a mere innocence in civil concerns; they boast their services to the constitution, to the episcopal church, and to the family of their king, as recorded by historians; and have been so little inclined to undue demands in their own favour, that they have suffered their obvious rights for many years to rest unclaimed.

That the instance, even in this speculative age, scarcely exists of a Dissenter being a republican, and much less of his being desirous to risk a convulsion for a change in our present happy constitution; that in their political opinions they differ from each other like other Englishmen; resembling other Englishmen in this also, that while denied redress they will never cease to make complaint.

That while the sacramental test is a profanation of a holy rite, inconclusive as to the general systems of the partaker, a barrier against the conscientious alone, and enforced by penalties the most disproportionate to the pretended offence; it is a departure also from the genuine purposes of civil government, which only require tests of a political and moral nature.

That as the sacramental test cannot legitimately be replaced by any other religious test; so neither are any sectaries to be singled out as the objects even of civil tests, on account of religious opinions, if free from a mischievous civil operation.

That as concord among people of different religious persuasions is proved by many examples, to be not only possible, but natural, wherever the civil power gives to each its protection; so the modern prevalence of liberal opinions makes it a folly to expect that the Dissenters will continue deprived of their rights, without subjecting the public to a renewal of their claims as long as they remain resisted.

That an immediate repeal of the test laws will dissipate the present union of the Dissenters, who have no other common bond than that of their common oppression.

That the Dissenters are too few to do mischief, if their claims are granted; and may easily be brought under restraint again, if they should abuse their liberty.

That the state is interested in increasing the number of its subjects, in extinguishing their ancient mutual aversions, in making every one of them easy, and in keeping up the persuasion at home, and the confession abroad, that no government is more happy than its own; which never can be the case if the state persists in religious oppressions, which so many other countries have abandoned with a politic disdain, from civil considerations.

That

That it is the duty of the civil power to weigh these positions, since if the right of private judgment is once established, the sectary has simply to plead the existence of that right, while the civil power is bound to prove the necessity of every infringement it makes in it; in short, it is the state which must explain its conduct upon these occasions, and not the sectary.

That the repeal of the present test laws in nothing concerns the clergy. It respects only the distribution of civil employments, for civil objects, by persons acting in civil capacities; and neither the religious opinions nor practice, and still less the powers, privileges, and revenues of the church can be in the least affected by a concession, in which if the clergy concur, they may render themselves popular in an age in which they are liable to a variety of attacks.

That the Dissenters in general have proposed to favour, at the next general election, the candidates who shall actually have *proved* themselves their friends, or whom they *believe* to be such; but say nothing of express *promises* as to the future; though, since election implies a choice on the part of the constituent, and since a general unalienable right, like that of liberty of conscience, is to be judged of, independent of any circumstances, the Dissenters might fairly ask for a promise; which the candidate on his side however, is no less at liberty to accede to or reject.

Such are the facts and positions which occur to me upon this important subject. The detail of them may be useful, as it will provoke many persons to think for themselves, or may occasion other persons to think for them. This last service, the perusal of a part of them only has actually performed, in the case of a person whose masterly pen will secure to itself more attention than is in the power of my warmest commendations to produce.

I shall conclude my present letter with inserting the remarks I allude to, which will easily point out their own reference to what has preceded.

DETACHED REMARKS.

' Excluding any description of men from serving their country,
' is no trivial injury, but the severest punishment, as well as the
' most mortifying stigma which the legislature can inflict.—The
' manners of the times have happily put an end to the corporal
' punishments imposed in consequence of religious opinions by
' the Inquisition. But civilization and improvement of men
' have made an opening for punishments which affect us
' deeply, in proportion as the mind is more feeling.
' Corporal punishment, fines, and imprisonment,
' they are the immediate acts of power;

'is itself a check upon them. But a general incapacitation is at
'once fundamental and comprehensive: its operation is silent,
'being applied to things, and not to persons: it gives room to no
'discussion, which the repeated trials of individuals would occasion,
'and must produce one of two consequences; it must make slaves
'of the dissenters, and must discourage them from taking any in-
'terest in public transactions; or else must render them turbulent,
'discontented, and consequently disaffected, and ready on all occa-
'sions to join any other descriptions of discontented men, to seek
'redress in common with them by their joint efforts.

' ' Every free government must be considered as instituted to pre-
'serve to every man the full right of exercising every faculty of
'mind and body, in any manner which does not prevent his fellow
'subjects from exercising equally their faculties; and their powers
'are in their nature limited to this end. Their institution is to pre-
'vent persecution, civil and religious, not to enforce either. It is
'therefore of the utmost consequence that government should shew
'the *necessity* of such an exertion of its power, in so great a viola-
'tion of right.—And if opinions make tests necessary, civil opinions
'should come under consideration before religious opinions, as they
'affect the conduct of men more immediately. Compare the opi-
'nions now prevailing in a neighbouring nation and the religious
'opinions professed for ages by the dissenters: which tend most
'to action?—But it is a mockery to suppose any necessity in the case,
'where the dissenters are suffered to make laws, which it is pre-
'tended that it is unsafe to let them assist in executing; notwith-
'standing it is well known that the greatest grievance under which
'our municipal government labours is, that the laws are not suf-
'ficiently enforced, but are ill executed for want of a proper choice
'of resident Magistrates. And if no *necessity* can be made apparent,
'it establishes a power totally void of principle, and alarming
'both to civil and religious liberty; and which may be carried to
'the most dangerous lengths.

' Though the corruption of the times has made several employ-
'ments in the State more lucrative than they ought to be, it is a
'most degrading principle to suppose that men have no higher
'motive than an undue lust of power or desire of profit, when they
'are ambitious only of a capacity of serving the public; and that
'the party in possession are therefore right in securing such emo-
'luments among themselves. It is to be hoped that in due time
'the emoluments of places will be reduced to their proper level.
'Necessity may carry this point, if public virtue does not; and
'the public should in the mean time be inspired with higher as well
'as truer motives to public action. Whatever motives may secretly
'govern the conduct of individuals, emoluments can never be suf-
' fered

'fered to come into question with honour and right: The tame surrender of either is incompatible with the spirit of freedom; and let a man be ever so indifferent about emolument, he stamps himself with the character of a slave, as long as he sits down contented under the deprivation of his most essential rights, and from a pretence (that of religion) calculated to excite his spirit, and never to depress it.

'Instead of checking reforms a denial must aid them, as it leaves a powerful standard, to which all reformers will necessarily resort, and will promote every tendency of the kind, unless the door is to be ever after shut to all reason and discussion, which, considering the character of the times, can only be considered as folly in the extreme.

'If the Dissenters are made easy, they are too few to do mischief; if their claims are rejected, they may prove to be too many.'

Here the *remarks* conclude, to the equal regret of the public and myself. Here then I shall rest this part of my subject, which I consider as containing the foundation of the claims of the Dissenters.—In a subsequent letter I shall consider the foundation of the opposite claims of the *clergy*.

A CHRISTIAN POLITICIAN.

II. *Letter of a Christian Politician.*

HAVING considered the claims of the Dissenters to a repeal of Test Laws, I shall now review the claims which the body of the clergy urge for their continuance; I say the body of the clergy; for they spare me the pain of conceiving this allusion to the majority of them to be invidious. That lead which they have always taken in this unhappy controversy, they are now resuming; and Mr. Pitt has avowed that his own fears on the subject, were originally and expressly suggested by the bishops. Besides, to neglect to assign them this post of honour, would imply a fear of questioning the validity of the pretensions of those, who ought to be most acquainted with the nature of religious disputes.

But where shall *any* set of men find a justification of their pretensions to examine into the religion of others?—To postpone for a moment the political part of our discussion, let us ask whether the clergy find any precept to this effect in *natural* religion; which, by its very essence, is defective as to positive precepts, and to presume to supply the want of which is in fact pretending to a revelation? So glaring a wrong therefore as the control of the religion of others, never can arise out of a right so imperfectly constituted, nor can the religion of nature ever speak contrary to the dictates of nature itself.—If natural religion is
silent,

silent, let us next take a rapid and summary view of the *words*, the objects, and the example of *Christ*.

He who said that his kingdom is not of this world; that we should call no man master; that the priestly Jew was inferior to Samaritans and sinners; that peace-makers and the persecuted for righteousness sake, are alike blessed; that after obeying God, nothing is more important than loving our neighbour; that we cannot at once serve God and Mammon; that the tares are not yet to be separated from the wheat, but that the sun rises alike on the evil and on the good; he who declared this, and that we should not judge lest we be judged, but forgive as we expect to be forgiven; has left nothing upon record by which any one shall say to another, ' I am worthier than thou ;' or ' that the things that are ' Cæsar's belong to those alone, who best know the doctrine of ' Christ, who yet denied that the things of Cæsar appertained to ' his followers.'—If possible, still more speaking are the *objects* of Christ and his *example*, than even his words. He found a confined and an exclusive religion, and he opened it to receive into it the fulness of the Gentiles; he attacked the Sanhedrim, lawyers, scribes and pharisees of his native country, (that is, its established clergy) and rejecting a hierarchy, he made use of fishermen for his own disciples; he fixed no creeds and no liturgy, but in lieu of them, gave a short prayer and general lessons of charity, accommodated to every good government; he had no alliance with the civil power, but finally fell a martyr to its interposition; instead of calling for legions of angels to vindicate his cause, he said, let the will of *God* be done; and knowing that his own religion could not be universal, while the doctrine of intolerance secured every where a local protection to each false religion, and a local exclusion to the true one, he bid all men be content with humbly inquiring into *themselves*, and to love even their enemies; instead of teaching them to inquire into the religion of their *neighbours*.—To *inquire* into the religion of our neighbours did I say? Is the Romish *inquisition* itself, more than a court of religious *inquiry* : It inquires in order actively to punish, and our English *Test* inquisitors inquire negatively in order to depress. If the degrees of the thing differ, let it be said in favour of Spain and Portugal, that so unhappily does their knowledge differ and form a proportionable excuse in their favour.—Such are the conclusions to be drawn from *religion* as it is taught by nature and by Christ, and which its proudest ministers cannot refute.

Having discovered the large scope left by religion, for variety in doctrine and in practice, let us next very briefly examine whether any boundaries to religious liberty are to be found in the *primary rights of men*; for that such rights exist, it is happily useless in this age to demonstrate. Among individuals what pretence has any man

to

to be a judge of my religious system, other than his fancy; for if mere opinion gives *him* authority to controul my opinion, it gives *me* a like title to controul his; which is making power the standard of truth, and rendering truth every where variable?—What then is to bring a question which private men cannot originally notice, before a civil tribunal, composed only of similar men, subject to similar difficulties? Was any aim at a general religious conformity, or any pious curiosity, to be reckoned amongst the great motives which first led us into civil society; or did not the fear rather operate of having our *liberty* with respect to religion invaded: for the first murder upon record was committed by the second man of our race upon his brother, while in the performance of a religious rite. To keep the *mind* free from the influence of force in concerns deemed to affect its temporal and eternal welfare, was an object no less important, than to keep the *body* free; for all know in how great a degree our happiness is seated in the mind:—And shall the civil magistrate then be supposed, so destitute of sagacity and resources, as not to know how to accomplish this great object of protecting religious sects from the injuries of one another, without giving to persons of one sect a power to depress every other? Does he not give a sufficient preponderance, when he makes every other sect tributary to the support of the particular ministers and churches of that sect, which he principally favours? If the magistrate's accession to power *depended upon his invention* in keeping men in mutual religious peace, without showing undue preferences or aversions to any, we should soon find him master of this simple secret; which consists merely in doing nothing; in noticing religion no otherwise than by protecting it; and in ceasing himself, in his public capacity, to be one of the disputants.—Speculative legal writers say, that the rights of property are the creature of civil laws, and yet all men appear greatly to respect these rights, though only *artificial*: but how much more is the right of conscience to be respected, which is personal and internal, and therefore *natural*; which may be enjoyed without injury to any; and which is never checked without doing mutual mischief to the oppressor and the oppressed.—Unhappy man! a being incapable of independence without civil government, and yet prostituting civil government so as to deprive himself of that better independence which it was meant to procure him.

But men, it is said, when, quitting a state of nature for civil society, enter upon *new relations* springing out of the new bearings and aspects incident to a social situation.—To this doctrine, in the hands of men honestly seeking the interests of civil society as taught by a *direct* contemplation of its nature, I would readily assent; but this system must be qualified when assumed by others, who conceive

civil

civil government to be a property, and men to be destitute of every privilege not imparted to them at the caprice of their rulers.—Let us therefore insist, first that civil society must at least aim at the same object that led men to its original adoption, namely, the happiness of the concerned. Secondly, that civil society must violate no private right, and least of all our more important private rights, unless for the general good. Lastly, that this general good must be evident and even transcendent, to compensate for any deviation from *so clear a guide to just government*, as is afforded by a retrospect to the primary rights of men.—By these rules let us try the case of excluding harmless sectaries from their mere eligibility to a share in the executive departments of society, solely on account of their opinion respecting a being who is placed in another world. The best argument certainly for such exclusion is the hope of preventing religious troubles: but to refute this argument, let us repeat our former remark, that statesmen would soon cease to be at a loss for more pacific methods of producing peace, if the discovery of such were once made a condition and test of their *own* eligibility to civil stations.

Let us now enquire whether the *clergy* have any proofs on the subject under debate, that remain as yet to be noticed.

I shall dwell little upon Dean *Swift*'s defence of the sacramental test. Even the bigotted Dr. Johnson, when speaking of this work says, ' The reasonableness of a test is not hard to be proved, ' but perhaps it must be allowed that the proper test has not been ' chosen.'—But happily an experimental confutation of these writers is afforded in Ireland, where the test law has been some time repealed without a single bad effect: on the contrary, it has apparently tended to prevent the Irish dissenters from catching the flame of reform so widely spread in other parts, and joining their own to the other discontents rankling in that kingdom. So profound a quiet has followed it, that the great body of Irish dissenters who had long acquiesced in their situation as it stood before the repeal, were almost as ignorant of the repeal having occurred, as they were before little attentive to the original restraint having existed.—Chance has thus spared our government the task of supporting in Ireland, as well as here, a very dangerous misconception of the clergy; for as the clergy will not distinguish that the dissenters here have in view their rights infinitely more than their interest, and are seeking a capacity of serving in offices rather than the offices themselves; so in Ireland, the same clergy might have esteemed themselves equally sagacious in preferring that conclusion respecting the views of the dissenters, which made least in favour of them.

Still

Still less notice shall I take of the performances of Bishop *Sherlock* respecting the Test Act, who it is insinuated, from some cause or other, did not continue to the last perfectly satisfied with what he had written †. The forcible logic with which he was answered by bishop Hoadly and others, must necessarily convince rational christians, that his *religious* arguments are fitter for Spain than for England; and his *political* arguments will be found to admit of easy refutation.—The high church writings of that age (in consequence of the change which has since taken place in the stability of the executive power, as well as in the temper and number of the dissenters, and in the opinions of mankind) having become in a good measure *obsolete*, it is matter of surprize with what profusion they are now re-published and dispersed; as if the church was best to be defended by the dead; its living dignitaries, during a controversy of three years, unless incidentally or perhaps anonymously, having published but little; and the *modern* principles urged by the dissenters being rather aspersed and vilified, than contested and debated. Is not this feature of the times symptomatic of an important change of opinion in many of the abler clergy?

I must treat bishop Warburton with somewhat more detail than either dean Swift or bishop Sherlock; his opinions being singular, little read though often referred to, and hitherto I believe never answered. The title of his work on the *alliance of church and state* has served to circulate a political tenet (namely that there is such an alliance) which his followers have conceived to be too useful, to suffer the fate of it to depend upon proofs; and very prudently so, for the bishop's system can only be supposed proved by those to whom it is difficult to understand it. The absurdity and indecency of it is such, that when it is rendered intelligible in words, the reader will be doubtful of their signification, and rather suspect his own understanding for a moment than the fair meaning of the bishop: but I pledge my character for the justice of the following account of

Bishop Warburton's System.

RELigious impressions (says this author) being found insufficient of themselves to restrain mankind, civil institutions are called to their aid, and by means of the two together, good order among men is established. Thus society exists under the influence of two

* 'Bishop Sherlock did not approve of his own writings against Bishop Hoadly
' (on the subject of the test and corporation acts,) and in his latter years, told a
' friend that he was a young man when he wrote them; and he would never
' have them collected into a volume.' See the first Edition of the Biographia Britannica, vol. 6, part 2, 1776, article Sherlock, Appendix to the Supplement.—
See also the Life of Bishop Sherlock prefixed to the 6th edition of his Discourses, p. 72.

principles, namely the one religious and the other political, each being originally and completely independent of the other, yet each profiting by a certain intermixture. The national church therefore, which is composed of the majority of the nation, avails itself both of its independence and of its services, to enter into a free alliance with the very same majority which composes the body politic; (that is, it enters into an alliance with itself.) By the terms of this alliance, it is said, the church obtains an endowment to render it independent of its flock, with a seat in parliament for its bishops (in order that the laws may not operate upon any who are not consulted) and likewise spiritual courts for inforcing strictness of manners: and the state obtains, a supremacy over the church, with a power of regulating the meetings of its synods and of preventing the excommunication of the members of the church, unless by its assent.—This compound establishment of church and state (he maintains) requires a security to be given by all public officers for their good behaviour to each respectively; in default of which, they must be excluded from their posts; since it would be deplorable for a church containing the majority, to find its enemies partaking in that magistrature, to which it has surrendered its own supremacy. As every sect (concludes our author) aims at superiority, peace requires an exclusive establishment for the largest sect; and a toleration at the same time ought to follow for other sects; since the cognizance of the civil power over religion, respects it only so far as religion is *useful*, and by no means as it is *true*.

Commentary and Conclusion.

Such is the scheme of Bishop Warburton, the fundamental principle of which has resounded in pulpits, been disseminated in pamphlets, and referred to in parliament; a scheme, which assumes liberal data in order to arrive at despotic conclusions, and which is too particular in its application to be founded upon general principles. But it is not in such cobwebs, however insidiously woven, that the rights of men are to remain entangled, as I trust will appear from the following remarks.—And first, it is curious to observe that, although the bishop cites Gulliver, Hobbes, and his own divine legation of Moses, in support of his opinions; yet his work, which so essentially respects religion, contains only three texts of scripture; and these texts are literally adduced to prove, that the pretensions of religion are neither temporal nor exclusive. The clergy seem indeed of late jealous of appeals to the bible, which sectaries understand perhaps as well as themselves; but our author candidly declares " a church by law established to be simply " a *politic* league and alliance with the state, for mutual support " and defence," and wholly independent of religious sanction.— But the bishop, it must be added, is guilty of a gross inconsistency

in

in defining the church to be " a religious society consisting of the whole body of the community, both laity and clergy," while he constantly argues upon it as if it consisted of the clergy solely, separate from and even opposed to the laity. That is, when he is establishing the title of the church to power, he refers us to its great majority; but when this power is once considered as granted, he then thinks only of the benefits which the clergy are to derive from it—Again, his sophistry in representing that the majority of the nation when under the character of the church, is distinct from the very same majority when under the character of the civil government, with a view to prove that it exhibits two independent powers capable of entering into a contract each with the other, seems to be a deliberate scoff at human understanding. We admit of religious mysteries with reverence where they are supposed to rest upon a divine authority; but I trust we shall never allow men to make use of their *own* mysteries as a title on which to found their *own* usurpations.—As to the sarcasm of our author, who says that the copy of the treaty for the union of the two societies civil and ecclesiastical, is kept in the same archive with the famous original compact between magistrate and people: I answer, that the latter compact is safely locked up in the following dilemma: viz. " The social compact either actually exists; or if it does not exist, the people may at any time say that it *shall* exist, for the reason that it *ought* to exist." And a nation may in like manner say to a clergy, as to any other body of its servants, that they shall subsist on such terms as the nation approves; or if they refuse to accede to these terms, it may dismiss them for others of more reasonable pretensions.

Let us however no longer speak at a distance upon this important subject of a church establishment.—Men may establish religious *doctrines,* or they may establish *funds* for supporting the teachers of religious doctrines; and either of these separately or both united, may be called a religious establishment. I shall not meet with much serious opposition, if I hold it of more importance to establish funds, than to establish doctrines. Doctrines change frequently, as indeed they ought to do, according to the reigning opinions of a nation; while the funds when once appointed, remain for many centuries, through all vicissitudes of men and things, giving stability to doctrines.—Shall the funds so established then, be appropriated for the support of religion under the direction of each contributor, as is seen in America; or shall the majority employ these funds as in Europe, in the support of that religion only which the majority professes? The first is a just and generous plan; and even the second plan is readily acquiesced in, especially where the sectaries are few and religious liberty is otherwise compleat, as being ultimately only a matter of pecuniary consideration.—But view the

matter

matter as we please, the clergy (who by the by are represented as averse to their *natural* alliance with their respective congregations) can surely find no grounds in either of these cases for their *pretended* free alliance with the state. It is true, the clergy benefit the state; but are they not paid for doing so; and do not the public then acquire a right to their utmost services, especially as being the source of all their public power which is solely communicated for this public end? Are not the clergy in this respect, like military persons by whom the state is defended, or like judges by whom its laws are administered, or like tutors by whom its youth is instructed? And shall military persons, shall judges and the instructors of youth, because their offices are each important to the state, say that they are primarily independent of it, and therefore intitled to a free alliance with it; and that if the state should pretend to alter their establishments or receive other persons into favor, a contract would be broken.—In the same sense and in the same degree that *any* of these professions is affirmed to be allied with the state, so are all the others of them; and no less so is every citizen, and even the chief magistrate himself. Each are allied, for each are under a contract of reciprocal duties: the state is for each, even for the meanest; and each even the greatest, is for the state: the community in short existing only by the operation its parts.

But even admitting a peculiar alliance between church and state, both of them combined cannot have power to do that which is wrong.——The connection with religion is meant to be useful, and not detrimental to society: it is designed to combine men, and not to divide them; and to lend efficacy to the power appointed to protect good citizens, and not to bewilder and stimulate it to acts of persecution. If civil government therefore is founded on the union of all for the benefit of all, it is highly improper wantonly to exclude any from eligibility to a share in the executive government; since this is to abridge the rights of the excluded subject, to damp his emulation, to vex him with unmerited reproaches, and perhaps to alienate his affections; while at the same time it curtails the privileges of those (whether it be the sovereign or people) who have the right of nominating to offices, as well as robs the state of the services of some valuable citizens. To found such exclusion upon religious pretences, is not only a great impertinence towards the deity, but a transgression of the just rules of human government. Sectaries are generally speaking, zealous and moral men; but even were it otherwise, religious test laws will not improve men, but must tend to make hypocrites of sectaries, and pharisees of the clergy. Place a confidence in the sectary and he pays his taxes willingly, whether to support a religious establishment from which he differs, or a civil

establish-

establishment in the emoluments and honours of which his connections seldom allow him to share in a due proportion: but stigmatize him, and you league him with his brethren and with strangers, and make him a clog upon administration; and what is infinitely more serious, you provoke him to turn critic and author; and sometimes becoming a succesful one, he changes the the sentiments of a whole nation both in church and in state

This period seems fast approaching.—Administration have suffered *religious* persons to dictate a conduct for them upon the present *political* question; and the first consequence has been, that the dissenters have joined the opponents of that administration. A second consequence is, that the dissenters by studying the subject of liberty in all its relations, are making themselves wonderfully perfect in general principles, and in the application of them to questions of church and state; and as religious liberty is become a subject to attract the notice of able writers at home and abroad, lights will multiply from every quarter. Whoever also is an enemy to tythes and spiritual courts, to the unequal distribution of church livings and the manners of the clergy, or to the present liturgy or church articles, will naturally join the dissenters against the church, if the dispute shall be continued; and this will be a third consequence.—And what have the clergy to gain by the intemperate part which they have themselves taken and have induced administration to take? Instead of intimidating the dissenters, the dissenters are inclined rather to ask more, than to ask less than they set out with; and have resolved to renew their application till they are succesful. If the church refuse to suffer the dissenters to be relieved in a point of justice, the church will probably shortly be obliged to undergo the still greater labour of reforming itself. In short, like pers ns born to great estate, indolent in habit or contemptuous in manner, they began with despising or vilifying their opponents, and they have already found the truth of the Italian adage, that *there is no little enemy*. Trusting to the maxims which answered in bigotted times, they have pursued these maxims in times little suited to their reception. Deceived by the ready obedience of their numerous adherents, founded in misconception and habit, they conceive that this obedience will be permanent in spite of the progress of information. In short, they look for success rather from force than from prudence; from clamour rather than conciliation; forgetting that in an age of revolutions, to abandon in time what is wrong, is the best way to secure what is right; and that they are giving up a powerful opportunity of attaching sectaries, when they forbid administration to acquire the means of alluring them with places. They disgrace Christ's religion also, by supposing that it can only be accommodated to the good pur-

poses

poses of society, under one single form of it in each country where it is introduced. And instead of agreeing with bishop Warburton, that the state is interested in no religious dogma, except the being and providence of God, and the difference between good and evil, they enter into a thousand peculiarities, and seek to change a *practical civil* government into a *controversial religious* one. If I were to name however the circumstance which has done the clergy least credit in the present contest, it is their want of judgment and information; which has proceeded so far, that they have usually rested the claim to civil employments upon the law of the strongest; that is, they have made it the lion's share.—Their irritability respecting the political history of sectaries is peculiarly unfortunate, if we consider the conduct of the major part of the English established clergy since the Norman conquest. Did not this clergy for example play the tyrant both over subjects and kings, acknowledge a foreign supremacy, grasp at all property till the laity checked possessions in mortmain, invade the province of lawyers, oppose the reformation with fire and gibbets, support the Stuarts, obstruct the revolution, countenance several rebellions against the reigning family, and shew such a temper in their convocations that the crown has never of late permitted their sittings?—If the established clergy persist in appealing to *history* against sectaries, it is thus they will lay themselves open to retorts: But this criterion is too false and invidious for either party to resort to, since (little as the clergy seem to take merit in it) mankind have certainly changed for the better in modern times, and are solely to be judged of by their individual overt-acts, according to general political rules, without reference either to their religion or ancestors.—I shall not dwell upon the *dissimilarity* of the church constitution from our happy civil constitution: this and other dormant questions will gradually wake to public notice, if the dissenters are resisted; since acting like a little leaven upon the minds of others, oppressed men gradually raise an extensive ferment; for plausible principles, actively urged and properly directed, have never failed to make a contagious impression upon institutions which are vulnerable in themselves, and whose reformation has promised liberty and plunder to many.—I shall only observe that those who conceive that *every* sect aims at pre-eminence as a body, not only contradict facts observed in other nations, where many sects are known to be perfectly indifferent to it; but they seem too probably to judge of the ambition of others from what they find in themselves.

But I have now done with the clergy, I mean that part of the clergy which is at present so active; for happy am I to know, that there are many amiable and splendid characters in the church, who view with a silent anxiety the present proceedings of its majority, and to whose moderation and superior sense the rest will probably

be

be indebted hereafter for a shelter from the storm, which as yet is only approaching.

To these enlightened persons, to the laity and to the legislature, I address the hints which follow. First, If numbers in favor of an establishment are beneficial to the church or state, then in proportion as the tenets of it are few, simple, and general in their nature, the more persons will it comprehend and the fewer will it exclude. Secondly, The few persons so excluded, instead of being forced to become enemies by being treated as such, will be conciliated by a due proportion of places, honors, and confidence, being conferred upon them; and it should be remembered that the influence of sectaries does not rest so much upon their numbers, as upon their arguments, unanimity, and zeal. Lastly, no punishments or legal disabilities should be inflicted upon any for religious doctrines or practices, unless such have likewise a political operation; and in order to distinguish in what degree their nature is political, it will in general be found an infallible criterion, to consider in what light they would appear in a state in which all religion whatever should be unknown or at least unnoticed.—If this be not the language of plain, practical sense, I will renounce the character of

A CHRISTIAN POLITICIAN.

APPENDIX No. I.

The Case of the Protestant Dissenters, in Relation to the Laws by which the Sacramental Test is imposed, 1790.

Corporation Act. 13 Car. II. Sess. 2. c. 1.   IN the year 1661 a statute was made, intituled, *An Act for the well governing and regulating of Corporations.* This statute, after empowering the king to appoint commissioners for removing and displacing any persons who, upon the 24th day of December, 1661, should be mayors, aldermen, recorders, bailiffs, town-clerks, common-councilmen, and other persons then bearing any office of magistracy, or places or trusts or other employments relating to the government of cities, corporations, and boroughs, and cinque-ports, and their members, and other port-towns;— provides and enacts, "That from and after the ex-"piration of the said commissions*, no person shall for ever here-"after be placed, elected, or chosen in or to any the offices or places "aforesaid that shall not have, within one year next before such elec-"tion or choice, taken the sacrament of the Lord's Supper, accord-"ing to the rites of the church of England;— and in default hereof, "every such placing, election, and choice, is hereby enacted and "declared to be void."

By statute 5 Geo. I. c. 6. § 3. an officer offending against the corporation act is rendered irremovable, unless a prosecution be commenced against him, within six months after his election.

Test Act. 25 Car. II. c. 2. § 2. 5.   In the year 1672, a statute was made, intituled, *An Act for preventing Dangers which may happen from Popish Recusants,* by which it is, among other things, enacted, "That every person that shall be admitted, entered, placed, or taken "into any office, civil or military; or shall receive any pay, salary, "fee, or wages, by reason of any patent or grant of his Majesty; or "shall have command or place of trust from or under his Majesty, "his heirs or successors, or by his or their authority, or by autho-"rity derived from him or them within this realm of England, "domi-

---

* These commissions expired on the 25th of March, 1663; and more extraordinary commissions, it is probable, were never issued. The powers given to the commissioners were 'new, and unknown to the constitution, which nothing 'but the most urgent necessity, real or imaginary, could have justified: *for they 'were empowered, among other things, at their will and pleasure, to remove all 'corporation officers, if they should deem it expedient for the public safety, and at their 'will and pleasure to fill up all vacancies occasioned by such removals or otherwise.*' See Sir Michael Foster's argument in the Court of the Judges Delegates, in the case of Allen Evans, Esquire, against the Chamberlain of London, in the Appendix to Dr. Furneaux's Letters to Sir William Blackstone, No. 1.

"dominion of Wales, or town of Berwick upon Tweed; or in his Majesty's navy; or in the several Islands of Jersey and Guernsey; or that shall be admitted into any service or employment in his Majesty's houshold or family; shall receive the sacrament of the Lord's Supper, according to the usage of the church of England, *within three months* after his admittance in, or receiving his said authority and employment, in some public church, upon some Lord's day immediately after divine service and sermon: — And

Penalty. "that every person that shall neglect or refuse to take the sacrament as aforesaid, and yet, after such neglect or refusal, shall execute any of the said offices or employments, and being thereupon lawfully convicted, *shall be disabled to sue or use any action, bill, plaint, or information, in course of law, or to prosecute any suit in any court of equity;* or TO BE GUARDIAN OF ANY CHILD; *or executor or administrator of any person; or capable of any legacy or deed of gift; or to bear any office; and shall forfeit the sum of five hundred pounds, to be recovered by him or them that shall sue for the same.*"

By statute 9 Geo. II. c. 26. § 4. the time within which persons being beyond the seas are required to receive the sacrament of the Lord's Supper, according to the usage of the church of England, in pursuance of the last mentioned act, is enlarged to *six calendar months* after their return to, or arrival in England: And by statute 16 Geo. II. c. 30. § 3. the time for all persons in office to receive the sacrament of the Lord's Supper, according to the usage of the church of England, is enlarged to *six months* after their admittance in, or receiving their authority or employment.

The protestant dissenters have long felt themselves aggrieved by the requisition of the sacramental test, as a qualification for admission to civil and military offices; and from this grievance they humbly hope to be relieved, for the following reasons:

I. The sacrament of the Lord's Supper, having been solemnly appointed by our Blessed Saviour only for the remembrance of his death, ought not to be applied to civil purposes.

II. Every man hath an unalienable right, as it is now generally acknowledged, to judge for himself in matters of religion; and as the dissenters have always proved themselves well affected to the present government, and have been ever ready to take the oaths required by law, it is unjust and oppressive to deprive them of civil rights, only on account of their scruples to receive the sacrament as a civil test.

III. The receiving of the Lord's Supper occasionally, according to the usage of the church of England, is no proof of an approbation of the whole constitution and frame of that church, since many christians conform in this particular, who do not approve of other parts of the establishment; and other christians, as well as unbelievers, may

comply

comply with this ceremony, merely for interested or ambitious purposes. Such a test, therefore, can be no real security to the church of England.

IV. The repeal of the laws, by which the sacramental test is imposed, would not injure the established church. That church was established long before the imposition of this test, and would continue to be established, although it should be removed. By such repeal the doctrine, discipline, privileges, and revenues of the church would not be in the least affected: and many serious clergymen would find, in the alteration, ease to their consciences, and safety from vexatious prosecutions; for although the church of England forbids notorious blasphemers of God, slanderers of his word, adulterers, fornicators, drunkards, and other offenders, to come to the holy table, yet if the minister should refuse, upon requisition, to admit such persons to the sacrament, to qualify them for offices, he may be harrassed by expensive civil prosecutions.

V. In no other country is the sacramental test required as a qualification for civil employments; and it must be particularly remarked, that episcopalians in North Britain, who are dissenters from the church established there, are not liable to any incapacities in consequence of not qualifying themselves by receiving the sacrament according to the usage of that church, but have free admission to all the offices in Scotland, upon taking the usual oaths: And yet in England the natives of Scotland belonging to the establishment of that country (among whom episcopalian dissenters are so liberally treated) cannot be members of the privy council, or hold any commission in the army or navy of Great Britain, to the support of which they contribute their proportion, without receiving the sacrament according to the rites of a church to which they do not belong. No history, ancient or modern, affords such an instance of the exclusion of a free people from offices which may so properly be called THEIR OWN.

VI. In the year 1779 an act was passed in Ireland, for the relief of his Majesty's faithful subjects the protestant dissenters of that kingdom, by which it is enacted, "That all and every person and " persons, being protestants, shall and may have, hold, and enjoy " any office or place, civil or military, and receive any pay, salary, " fee, or wages belonging to or by reason of such office or place, " notwithstanding he shall not receive, or have received the sacra-" ment of the Lord's Supper,—without incurring any penalties— " for or in respect of his neglect of receiving the same." This measure was designed to give additional security to the church of Ireland, by conciliating the protestant dissenters of that country: and it is apprehended that it had the desired effect. The protestant dissenters in England, therefore, cannot but consider it as ungenerous and unjust that they should be treated as enemies to the establishment here, when the friendship of their brethren has been acknowledged, and their assistance courted, by the establishment in the sister-kingdom; an establiment similar to that of the church of England.

VII. The absurdity of the test laws, as they now stand, is most glaring; for though a dissenter may be a legislator in either house of parliament, without receiving the sacrament according to the rites of the church of England, yet he cannot legally without it have any share in the direction of the Bank of England, the East-India, Russia, or South-Sea Companies; or be a custom-house officer or an exciseman; or hold the meanest corporation office in any city or borough. He may not, in some places, even assist in the management of hospitals or alms-houses, which he or his ancestors may have endowed.

VIII. The large and indefinite terms in which the test act is expressed, may give occasion to the grossest abuses, and render it an instrument of the most grevious persecution and oppression. If the act should be rigorously enforced, many protestant dissenters might be compelled to violate their consciences, or to abandon even the ordinary occupations by which they now support themselves and their families. The act is not confined merely to *public**   employments. It extends not only to persons who bear offices civil and military, but to those who have command or place of trust under his Majesty, *or by authority derived from him*. Those who scruple to receive the sacrament, according to the rites of the church of England, are not only prohibited from partaking of the bounty of the King, but from *receiving* any pay, salary, fee, or wages, by grant from the crown, in return for the most meritorious services! It has been questioned in a court of justice, whether censors†, appointed by the college of physicians, were not obliged to qualify; and the point seems to be still undetermined. It was not settled till the reign of his late Majesty, that the common burgesses and freement‡ of a corporation, who do not exercise any office relating to the government thereof, were exempted from this act. In the year 1702 the House of Lords§ attempted,

---

* See Lords Journals, vol. XII. p. 567.
† Carthew's Reports, p. 478.——Modern Reports, vol. V. p. 431.
‡ Strange's Reports, vol. II. p. 828.
§ In the debate between the two Houses relating to the bill, the Lords said, "That the disagreeing to the clause relating to work-houses, where the poor were employed and relieved, seems very hard, since it could never be conceived, that the distribution of *fine Presbyterian bread to the poor*, and *Dissenting water-gruel to the sick*, could ever bring any prejudice to the church of England; especially by such as having no authority in the government, or profit by the administration of such charities, gave them indifferently to those of all persuasions." They farther said, "That the clause concernin gthose societies that are engaged in taking care of the poor—has no relation to *endowed* hospitals which are under peculiar statutes, and to which none of these people have any access, that the law has taken care of these, and secured them; and that this clause relates only to *free and voluntary* societies for such charaties, which the Lords do not think fit to put any restraints upon, or to bar any from coming into them." Chandler's Debates, vol. III. p. 230. 242.

APPENDIX.

attempted, but *in vain*, to procure, in the bill against occasional conformity, the insertion of a clause to exempt *free and voluntary hospitals*, though not endowed, out of the test act. And "so low have these holy things been prostituted," that Mr. Locke tells us*, "Men have been driven to take the sacrament *to obtain licences to sell ale.*"

IX. It is manifestly unjust, that the rights of innocent persons should be destroyed or affected by the criminal conduct or neglect of others; yet no man (if the objection be taken at the proper time†) can recover a debt in an inferior court, over which an unqualified corporator presides: nor can the election of a corporate officer, before magistrates who have neglected to qualify, be supported. It is not less unjust that punishment should be inflicted for crimes which the offender could not possibly know he was in a capacity to commit; yet, upon succeeding to an office of inheritance (as no entry is necessary) a person may suffer in consequence of the lapse of the six months before he has even notice of his right having accrued.

X. The penalties inflicted by the test act are enormous, and humility cannot contemplate them without horror. The party is not only deprived of the office, but he is incapaciated to sue in any court of law or equity; *to be guardian of any child*; to be executor or administrator of any person; to take any legacy or deed of gift; or to bear any office; and is besides subjected to forfeit five hundred pounds to any person who shall sue for the same: And as prosecutions under this act are not limited in respect of time, its operation having been only suspended occasionally during certain intervals by acts of indemnity, no person, *whether conformist or non-conformist*, who has been in office, and has omitted, through illness or mere inadvertence, to qualify according to law, can ever afterwards be safe.

XI. The situation of foreign countries with regard to Britain affords strong arguments for the repeal of these oppressive laws. To the intolerance of our neighbours, in former times, we owe the introduction or perfection of some of our most important manufactures; among others, those of wool and silk: and other nations may, in like manner, profit by the illiberality of this country. The United States of America, in addition to the ease with which they permit foreigners to become naturalized, make no distinctions as to religious sects in relation to their public offices. Other countries are gradually improving in their policy, in this particular. By the late commercial treaty with France, assented to by the same legislature

to

---

* In his second letter concerning toleration, last edition of his works, vol. II. p. 360.—and see his third letter, p. 531.——This circumstance was also mentioned by Sir Henry Capell, in the House of Commons. Grey's Debates, vol. IX. p. 111.

† See 2 Mod. 193, 194.···3 Lev. 184, 242.---Lord Raym. 885.

to which the protestant dissenters now apply, it is provided, "That in matters of religion the subjects' of the two crowns shall enjoy perfect liberty." and by the temper now discovered in that kingdom the fullest liberty appears likely to be confirmed to non-catholics; so that to many protestant dissenters it may be of little importance, as far as religion is concerned, in which of the two countries they and their families shall reside. Moreover in France, Germany, Prussia, Russia, Holland, Poland, and other countries, many persons dissenting from their respective establishments have been employed in the highest offices, who, by the most signal services, have manifested this important truth, THAT A DISSENTER FROM THE ESTABLISHED RELIGION OF A COUNTRY MAY BE A TRUE FRIEND TO ITS GENERAL INTERESTS AND PROSPERITY.

For these and other reasons, the dissenters are induced to renew their application to parliament for relief, humbly apprehending that their request will appear to be founded in justice, and that a compliance with it will redound to the honour of religion; will contribute to the welfare and security of the nation; will be honourable to the king, as the common father of his people, and no way injurious to any one subject in his majesty's dominions. Arguments so weighty and cogent as those which are now offered cannot fail, they trust, in conjunction with the enlarged and liberal spirit of the times, to procure from the legislature the repeal of statutes, which cannot be considered as in any degree grounded on public necessity, or public advantage.

APPENDIX No. II.

History of the Test and Corporation Act, "extracted from the Rights "the Dissenters to a compleat toleration, asserted." 2d Edit. 1789.

THE sacramental Test is used only in England. It was originally devised against papists, but from a gradual revolution in the principles of protestant dissenters, many of them becoming unable conscientiously to take it, it operated at last against them also.

The Sacrament of the Lord's Supper had been made a test of the principles of the communicant here, prior to the year 1571, which was long before any protestants had openly separated from the establishment.

The sacramental Test, thus solely destined against popish offenders, could not materially affect protestant dissenters, so long as, fettered by the prejudices of the times in which they lived, they thought it sinful to separate. Occasional conformity always existed between the different reformed churches, and in England it was co-
equal

APPENDIX.

eval with non-conformity itself. The old puritans were dreadfully afraid of falling into the crime of schism, and in 1587, one of the rules they imposed upon themselves was, that they should endeavour to wipe off the imputation of schism, inasmuch as *the brethren communicate with the church in the word and sacraments*, and in all other things, except their corruptions. The non-conformists in general continued to communicate, at least occasionally, until the year 1645, when the presbyterian form of worship was established. After the Restoration, and even after the act of uniformity, most of the presbyterians, and many of the other sects, communicated occasionally with the episcopal establishment.

Bishop Stillingfleet dates the entire separation of the dissenters from the church from the time of the King's declaration of indulgence, issued in the year 1671-2; in consequence of which they built some meeting-houses, and continued ever afterwards to keep up separate congregations.

If from the general prevalence of this practice after the Restoration, the Sacramental Test *could not* possibly operate against protestant dissenters, it may fairly be inferred, that the legislature had some other object in view when they imposed it. And when we recollect that it had long before made part of the penal laws against papists, we cannot entertain a doubt that its application, in this instance, was intended to be an addition of severity to those laws, under which the papists had long and grievously suffered.

To conciliate the affections of a people divided by religious distinctions, Charles the Second published the famous Declaration from Breda, copies of which he sent to the speakers of both Houses of Parliament, before he himself came over. Trusting to this assurance, the Presbyterians, notwithstanding a strong opposition from the other sects, entered heartily into his views, and compassed his restoration.

By means of the Restoration, the church of England was tacitly re established: But for some time afterwards the Presbyterian clergy were allowed to retain their livings; the King by proclamation stated his intention to have the liturgy revised, to which a strict conformity was not exacted; and of the numerous vacant bishopricks, several were not filled up. Attempts were made without success (in which the Presbyterians had good reason to complain of ill usage) to fix upon some discipline and form of worship that should include them and the friends of episcopacy in one national church. In 1661, while the terms of this comprehension, projected in pursuance of the King's declaration, were negociating, the Corporation Act passed. Mr. Hume gives the following account of this Act:
" During the violent and jealous government of the Parliament and
" of the Protectors, all magistrates liable to suspicion had been
" expelled the corporations, and none had been admitted who gave
" not

"not proofs of affection to the ruling powers, or who refused to "subscribe the covenant. To leave all authority in such hands, "seemed dangerous; and therefore the Parliament empowered the "King to appoint commissioners for regulating the corporations, "and expelling such magistrates as either had obtruded themselves "by violence, or professed principles dangerous to the constitution, "civil or ecclesiastical."

It appears that the Corporation Act originated in the House of Commons, and that when it was sent up to the Lords it did not contain the clause requiring persons elected to corporate offices to take the sacrament; the preamble only briefly stating, "that the suc- "cession in corporations might be most probably perpetuated in the "hands of persons well affected to his Majesty, and the established "government." At first the Lords new modelled the whole of the bill; endeavouring, for instance, like true friends of despotism, to make this temporary expedient a "perpetual change." After several conferences, the Lords gave up or altered all these objecti- onable clauses; but unfortunately, when the bill had been nearly five months under consideration of the two Houses, and after two con- ferences they were nearly agreed, an adjournment took place. When they met again it should seem that the clause which imposed the Sacramental Test, and was the only part of the bill not of a temporary nature, was proposed in the House of Lords with other amendments; and the Commons having afterwards agreed to those amendments, the bill was passed. Thus the clause in question, so far from being a principal, or even collateral object of either House of Parliament, was not so much as thought of till after they had had two conferences upon the other parts of the bill; and after its general scope had been perfectly settled. Few can doubt against whom this clause was levelled; for, up to that time, the sacrament had been designed as a test for persons addicted to popery only; and protestant dissenters were *then* almost universally communicants in the church.

The Act did not require the Sacrament to be taken in the church of England as it was *then* established, but as it should be settled nearly two years afterwards; when it might reasonably be expected the comprehension would have taken place.

The crown having gained a vast accession of strength by the Cor- poration Act, no measures were afterwards kept with the Presbyte- rians. The memory of their past services, or of the King's solemn promise, no longer operated in their favour; all hopes of a compre- hension vanished;—and the Act of Uniformity disgraced the annals of England. By that Act they received a deadly blow; and more than two thousand of their ministers, who could not conscientiously comply with the terms of conformity, were driven from their livings. "This Bill," as the elegant historian before cited remarks, "rein- "stated

APPENDIX.

"stated the church in the same condition in which it stood before the commencement of the civil wars; and, as the old persecuting laws of Queen Elizabeth still subsisted in their full rigour, and new clauses of a like nature were now enacted, all the King's promises of toleration, and of indulgence to tender consciences, were thereby eluded and broken."

Charles the Second was himself secretly of the Roman Catholic religion; and by treating the Non-conformists with severity, he hoped to obtain a toleration for those who professed it. On the other hand, the majority of every House of Commons throughout this reign had a rooted hatred and dread of popery, and although at the beginning of the first Parliament, they fell in with the resentments of the King and church, yet in a few years they discovered their error, and the danger to which they exposed the nation. The latter part of this reign was therefore passed in continual disputes between the House of Commons and the Crown; the latter struggling hard to protect Papists from persecution, the former pressing for further severities against them.

To secure the Non-conformists, he issued a proclamation (dated the 15th of March, 1671) suspending, by a dispensing power usurped as inherent in the royal prerogative, all the penal laws; and granting to the protestant Non-conformists public places of worship; to papists, the freedom of religion in their own houses.—This usurpation of absolute power, roused the drooping spirit of liberty; and the common danger united Protestants of all denominations. The dissenters accepted the indulgence; but provoked the resentment of the Court, by reprobating the exercise of prerogative which gave it.

Several members having, in the committee for forming the first address against the declaration of indulgence, expressed a strong desire, that the protestant Dissenters might have a legal instead of an unconstitutional toleration;—a bill was, on the 14th of February, 1672-3, ordered *nemine contradicente*, to be brought in, for the ease of Protestant Dissenters; and a day appointed to consider of the subject matter of it in a committee of the whole House. The bill passed the House of Commons, but the Lords making some amendments, a conference took place; and while the Commons were debating upon the report, a message came from the King requiring their *immediate* attendance in the House of Peers; and he ordered them to adjourn till the 20th of October following. This was on the 29th of March, 1673, when he was come to give the royal assent to the Test Act; and this interruption seems to have been the effect of contrivance, for the debate was so suddenly broken in upon by the black-rod knocking at the door, that the Commons had not time even to put the question of adjournment. The committee of the whole House reported the heads of the bill for the ease of Protestant Dissenters, on the 27th of February 1672;—and on the day after, it was resolved, *nemine contradicente*, that an address should be presented to his Majesty for suppressing the growth of popery.

In the mean time the bill for incapacitating papists was not forgotten. The Test Act was read the first time on the 5th of March; and such was the expedition used, that it was read a second time the next day, and passed and sent up to the Lords on the 12th of that month. In order to secure this bill, the supply was delayed: and the event shewed that this precaution was not unnecessary; for the bill for ease of the Dissenters, which was brought in *before* the Test Act was thought of, being postponed till the King had got a supply, was thereby lost.—The moderation with which the Dissenters conducted themselves in this awful crisis gained the affection and confidence of the House of Commons, whose constant endeavour was ever afterwards to screen them from the vengeance of a disappointed tyrant. The Dissenters who were members of the House of Commons, heartily concurred in passing an act which then affected very few of their brethren, and to which, however indefensible it may be in its principle, we are perhaps indebted for the portion of liberty we now enjoy. The political disorders of the state were far advanced, and violent remedies were held necessary to work a cure. Some of the Court party had endeavoured to persuade them to press forward the bill for ease of the Protestant Dissenters, hoping to occasion a breach between them and the House of Commons; but, in answer to these insidious attempts, Alderman Love, one of the members for the city of London, and one of the very few Dissenters who scrupled to receive the sacrament according to the rites of the church of England, declared in the debate, that it was his wish that " an effectual security might " be found against popery, and that nothing might interpose till " that was done: when that was over, the Dissenters would try to " deserve some favour, but at present they were willing to lie under " the security of the laws, rather than clog a more necessary work " with their concerns." Whether the Dissenters upon this occasion acted *wisely* may be disputed; but that they acted *generously* in thus disdaining the offers of the Court, and preferring a continuation of their sufferings under penal laws, to an unconstitutional exemption from them, no one can deny.

The effect of the Test Act was instantly felt in every department of government. The Duke of York resigned his office of Lord High Admiral, and Lord Clifford, then Lord High Treasurer, with other Roman Catholics about the court, followed his example; but so little did it operate against Protestant Nonconformists, that there is not the smallest trace in history of even *one* of their number vacating an office in consequence of it.

The

APPENDIX.

The House of Commons met, after a long adjournment, on the 20th of October 1673, and continued in the same favourable disposition towards the Dissenters. A bill was ordered in, " for a " General Test, to distinguish between Protestants and Papists: " *and those that shall refuse to take it to be uncapable to enjoy any of-* " *fice, civil or military;* or to sit in either House of Parliament; or to " come within five miles of the court, and a Committee appointed " to prepare it." From this title, or rather instruction to the Committee, the object of the bill must have been to repeal the Test Act, and to fix upon some more general Test for admission to offices, which should exclude the Roman Catholics, but should not affect Protestant Dissenters.—The Parliament being assembled in January, 1673; on the 21st of that month, the friends of the constitution introduced again the bill for a Test to distinguish between Protestants and Papists. Its title was now so altered, as to shew that the bill was meant also to encourage the prosecution of the latter. The Test proposed by this act was a declaration against popery, such as was afterwards made the qualification for a seat in Parliament. It was read twice and committed, but was lost by a prorogation, on the very day appointed for receiving the report of the Committee. In this manner the King frustrated, for the *second* time, the good intentions of the House of Commons towards the Dissenters, and at the distance of one hundred years their descendants have to complain that, to the disgrace of their country, they are still involved in an incapacity which was meant for others.

It is not my intention to enter further into the history of the Dissenters, that is immediately connected with the Sacramental Test. I shall therefore only observe in general, that the disposition of the House of Commons which passed the Test Act, and was dissolved in 1678-9, continued to the last favourable in the highest degree to the Nonconformists; and that one of the concluding acts of its political life was to provide a Test, which should allow Dissenters to sit in either House of Parliament, but should exclude Papists.

The heats occasioned by the Bill of Exclusion § continued to the end of this reign, and three successive Parliaments were dissolved

§ Through the reigns of Charles II. and James II. the church (says the same author) frequently gave support to the arbitrary designs of the court, even when they obviously tended to its destruction. The whole bench of Bishops (except three) voted against the Bill of Exclusion, and, as members of a Protestant establishment, endeavoured to secure a Papist for its head. A similar inconsistency of conduct was exibited in Scotland at the time of the Revolution: ' The Prelates of that kingdom, without, I believe a single exception, zealously adhered to the popish tyrant, and gave every opposition to their protestant deliverer. They met with their reward, for *their conduct* occasioned the abolition of Episcopacy in that country and the establishment of Presbyterianism in its room.

on

on its account.—In the year 1680, a feeble effort was made towards a comprehension of part of the Dissenters within the national church, but the bill for that purpose was dropped for one to relieve them from all the penal Acts made in the reigns of Elizabeth and James against Popish Recusants, which, by an extraordinary piece of political legerdemain, was not to be found, when it should have been presented for the royal assent.—At this period the resentment of the clergy against the Dissenters broke out afresh, and the King diligently nurtured the seeds of discord.—The friends of the Dissenters forming still a majority in the House of Commons, brought in a bill to repeal the Corporation Act, which was read a second time, and referred to a Committee. While this bill was depending, another came down from the Lords entitled, " An Act " for distinguishing Protestant Dissenters from Popish Recusants ;" which, for reasons given at large, Dr. Furneaux thinks had for its object the repeal of the Test Act. It does not appear that there was any opposition to either of these bills, but all proceedings upon them were ended by the sudden prorogation of Parliament. —The House of Commons, gaining a few minutes previous notice of the King's intention to prorogue them, contrived in a hasty manner to pass some resolutions on the state of the nation, and in favour of the Dissenters. These resolutions, made by the second House of Commons, after that which passed the Test Act, are an honourable testimony of the merits of the Dissenters, and shew that their services were not then forgotten. The Parliament was soon after dissolved by proclamation, and the Dissenters left for the remainder of this reign to the mercy of the King and the Church. Under their afflictions, however, they had this consolation, that they were supported by the best friends of the constitution, and were persecuted by the men, who brought Russel and Sydney to the scaffold. †

† In Ireland the Test Act was not introduced till the second year of Queen Anne, 1703. It pursued the terms of the English Test Act ; and all persons then in office, or who should be admitted before Easter Term 1704, were required to receive the Sacrament according to the usage of the church of Ireland, before the 1st of August 1706 ; and every person admitted after that day was to receive it within three months after his admittance. The subjects of Ireland were fortunate in another respect, for by the 6 Geo. I. c. 9. all prosecutions against this Act were to be commenced *within two years* after the admittance into office of the person prosecuted. The Test Act continued in Ireland, even with this mitigation, only *seventy-seven* years: in England it has been in force *one hundred and sixteen*.

APPENDIX.

APPENDIX No. III.

The following protests will shew the light in which the subject was considered at the time of its agitation a century ago.

Die Jovis, 21° Martii, 1688.

THE House having been in consideration of the bill for abrogating the oaths of allegiance and supremacy, and establishing others in their place.

A clause for repealing so much of the Test Act as concerns the receiving the sacrament was read.

And the question being put, whether to agree to the said clause? It was resolved in the negative.

Leave was given by the House to such Lords as will, to enter their dissents; and accordingly these Lords following, do enter their dissents, for the reasons following:

1st. Because a hearty union amongst protestants is a greater security to the church and state than any test that can be invented.

2dly. Because this obligation to receive the sacrament is a test on protestants rather than on the papists.

3dly. Because so long as it is continued, there cannot be that hearty and thorough union amongst protestants as has always been wished, and is at this time indispensably necessary.

4thly. Because a greater caution ought not to be required from such as are admitted into offices, than from the members of the two houses of parliament who are not obliged to receive the sacrament to enable them to sit in either house,

NORTH AND GREY,	DELAMER,	STAMFORD,
CHESTERFIELD,	GREY,	P. WHARTON.
J. LOVELACE,	VAUGHAN,	

Die Sabbati, 23° Martii, 1688.

Hodie 3a vice lecta est billa, An act for the abrogating of the oaths of supremacy allegiance, and appointing other oaths.

A rider (in parchment) providing, that no officer shall incur the penalties of the test act, in case he shall receive the sacrament in any protestant congregation within a year before or after his admission, was offered and read.

And

APPENDIX

And the question being put, whether this rider shall be made part of the bill?

It was resolved in the negative.

Leave was given to such lords as will, to enter their dissents, and these lords do enter their dissents in the reasons following:

1st. Because it gives great part of the protestant free men of England reason to complain of inequality and hard usage, when they are excluded from public employments by a law, and also because it deprives the king and kingdom of divers men fit and capable to serve the public in several stations, and that for a mere scruple of conscience, which can by no means render them suspected, much less disaffected to the government.

2dly. Because his majesty, as the common and indulgent father of his people, having expressed an earnest desire of liberty for tender consciences to his protestant subjects; and my lords, the bishops having, divers of them, on several occasions professed an inclination, and owned the reasonableness of such a christian temper; we apprehend, it will raise suspicions in mens minds of something different from the case of religion or the public, or a design to heal our breaches, when they find, that by confining secular employments to ecclesiastical conformity, those are shut out from civil affairs, whose doctrine and worship may be tolerated by authority of parliament, there being a bill before us, by order of the house, to that purpose; especially when, without this exclusive rigour, the church is secured in all her privileges and preferments, nobody being hereby let into them who is not strictly conformable.

3dly. Because to set marks of distinction and humiliation on any sort of men who have not rendered themselves justly suspected to the government, as it is at all times to be avoided by the makers of just and equitable laws, so may it be particularly of ill effect to the reformed interests at home and abroad in this present conjuncture, which stands in need of the united hands and hearts of all protestants, against the open attempts and secret endeavours of a restless party, and a potent neighbour who is more zealous than Rome itself to plant popery in these kingdoms, and labours, with his utmost force to settle his tyranny upon the ruins of the reformation all through Europe.

4thly. Because it turns the edge of a law (we know not by what fate) upon protestants and friends to the government, which was intended against papists, to exclude them from places of trust, as men avowedly dangerous to our religion and government; and thus the taking the sacrament, which was enjoyed only as a means to discover papists, is now made a distinguishing duty among protestant dissenters, to weaken the whole, by casting off a part of them.

5thly. Because mysteries of religion and divine worship are of divine original, and of a nature so wholly distant from the secular

affairs

affairs of public society, that they cannot be applied to those ends; and therefore the church, by the law of the gospel as well as common prudence, ought to take care not to offend either tender consciences within itself or give offence to those without, by mixing their sacred mysteries with secular interests.

6thly. Because we cannot see how it can consist with the law of God, common equity, or the right of any free-born subject, that any one should be punished without a crime: if it be a crime not to take the sacrament according to the usage of the church of England, every one ought to be punished for it, which nobody affirms: if it be no crime, those who are capable, and judged fit for employments by the king, ought to be punished with a law of exclusion, for not doing that which is no crime to forbear: if it be urged still, as an effectual test to discover and keep out papists, the taking the sacrament in those protestant congregations, where they are members and known, will be at least as effectual to that purpose.

| OXFORD, | MORDAUNT, | J. LOVELACE, |
| R. MONTAGUE, | P. WHARTON, | W. PAGET. |

APPENDIX IV.

Resolutions by the English House of Commons.

NOV. 6, 1680; Resolved, *nemine contradicente*, That it is the opinion of this House, that the acts of parliament made in the reigns of Queen Elizabeth and King James, ought not to be extended against Protestant Dissenters.

Jan. 10, 1680; Resolved *nemine contradicente*, That it is the opinion of this House, that prosecution of Protestant Dissenters upon the penal laws, is at this time grievous to the subject, *a weakening of the Protestant interest*, an encouragement to popery, and dangerous to the peace of the kingdom.

APPENDIX V.

Petitions of the Livery of London in 1689, to the House of Commons.

ON the 25th of June, 1689, Humphrey Edwin and John " Fleet, Sheriffs of the City of London and County of Middlesex, with Henry Cripe, Common Serjeant, presented a petition of the Citizens of London in Common-Hall assembled."

sembled, in which, among other matters, after stating "the im-
"portance of an *universal* amity and unity being preserved amongst
"the Protestant citizens;" and that "the principal danger im-
"pending over our English *church* and state, was from the *politic*
"popish designs to divide the protestants, as they did heretofore in
"the beginning of the reformation, whereby they first subdued and
"destroyed the Calvinists; and then, with the like blood thirsty
"cruelty suppressed the Lutherans, whom they had *deluded* to help
"them in the destruction of their Protestant brethren" "they pray
"that our most gracious King may be freed from all restraint of
"using his Protestant subjects indifferently in his military or civil
"services, according to their several qualities and abilities, where-
"with God Almighty, nature and experience have endowed them,
"to that very end that they might be useful to their King and
"country, and therein serve God in their generation."

APPENDIX VI.

Testimonies of our Kings respecting the Dissenters during more than a century.

THE declaration of Charles IId, sent from Breda, to both Houses of Parliament, to dispose them in favour of his restoration, is couched in these terms; "And because the passion and *uncharitableness of the times* have produced several opinions in re-
"ligion, by which men are engaged in parties and animosities against
"each other, which when they shall hereafter *unite in a freedom of*
"*conversation*, will be composed or better understood; We do de-
"clare, a liberty to tender consciences, and that no man shall be
"disquieted or *called in question* for differences of opinions in
"matters of religion, which do not disturb the peace of the king-
"dom; and that we shall be ready to consent to such an act of
"parliament, as upon mature deliberation shall be offered unto us
"for the full granting of *that* indulgence."

King William III, both in England and in Ireland, used his endeavours for this salutary purpose, which Charles IId had only promised. In England he declared from the throne as follows:

"*My Lords and Gentlemen,*
"Now I have the occasion of coming hither to pass this bill,
"which I hope will be for all our safeties, I shall put you in mind
"of one thing, which will conduce as much to our settlement, as
"a settlement will to the disappointment of our enemies. I am,
"with all the expedition I can, filling up the vacancies, that are
"in

" in offices and places of trust, by this late Revolution. I know
" you are sensible there is a necessity of some law, to settle the oaths
" to be taken by all persons to be admitted to such places. I recom-
" mend it to your care to make a speedy provision for it: and as I
" doubt not but you will sufficiently provide against papists, so I
" *I hope you will leave room for the admission of all protestants, that
" are willing and able to serve.* This conjunction in my service will
" tend to the better uniting you among yourselves, and the streng-
" thening you against your common adversaries.

In his answer to the address of the Irish House of Lords, he says: " His Majesty hopes that it will not be found inconsistent with
" the security of the established church, but on the contrary, will
" be looked upon as a means conducive thereto, to strengthen the
" protestant interest by rendering numbers of His Majesty's subjects
" here, who by the legal incapacities they now lie under are
" disabled from contributing to its support, more useful to his
" Majesty's service, and to the preservation of the *constitution both
" in church and state.*" And in his answer to the Irish house of commons are these words: " His Majesty is glad to find them sen-
" sible of the danger of the established church of Ireland from the
" great number of papists and other disaffected persons; hoping this
" consideration will incline them to enter upon such methods, as
" may make the Protestant Dissenters not only more easy, but more
" useful *to the support of the constitution both in church and state*;
" and will prove a great addition of strength to the protestant
" interest."

It is well known that Queen Anne was in the hands of the Tories, and endeavoured to keep the throne from the Hanover family; so that little more can be expected from her in favour of the Dissenters, than from James II.

George I. and II. were the known patrons of civil and religious liberty; and the liberal inclinations of the gracious prince now on the throne cannot be doubted, when it is considered how often he has declared himself to be the friend of the liberties of his people, that he has led his eldest son in particular to be friendly to revolution principles, and that he has assented to the establishment of the popish religion in Canada, to the increase of the religious liberty granted to the English Dissenting Ministers, and to a restoration of the Irish Dissenters to their civil rights.—It would be contrary to reason to suppose him adverse to the descendants of those, to whom his ancestors were so much indebted for the original acquisition and firm possession of the crown of these realms.

c APPEN-

APPENDIX Nº VII.

At a Meeting of the Committee for conducting the Application to Parliament, for a Repeal of the Test Laws, held at the King's Head Tavern, Poultry, London, Jan. 13, 1780, *Edward Jeffries, Esq. in the Chair:*

Resolved unanimously,

I. THAT the opinions and principles of the Protestant Dissenters have been proved by experience, and are well known to be perfectly congenial to the spirit of the free constitution secured to these kingdoms by the glorious Revolution, and friendly to the just authority of the monarchy, as established in the illustrious house of Brunswick, to which their loyalty and attachment have ever been conspicuously distinguished.

II. That every Test, calculated to exclude such men from civil and military offices on account of religious scruples, is a violation of their rights as men and citizens of a free state, inconsistent with the principles of the constitution of this country, and repugnant to the genuine spirit of true religion, subjecting a large number of deserving members of the state to a species of persecution not more injurious to them than dishonourable to the government of which they are useful and loyal subjects.

III. That exclusion from the enjoyment of civil rights, and incapacitation from holding offices of profit or honour, being a mode of punishment well known, in many instances, to our law, every exclusion partakes of the nature of punishment, and consequently of persecution, when applied to religious opinions.

IV. That the Sacramental Test of qualification to offices, which now stands established by law, is liable to this farther objection, which must greatly weigh in the minds of serious and religious men of all persuasions, that it is a profanation of a right held sacred in christian churches, by applying it to a purpose unconnected with religion, and repugnant to the pious object of its original institution.

V. That such a Test defeats the professed purposes of its own establishment, as from its nature it can only operate to exclude from offices the most sincere and conscientious men, while it leaves the door open to the profane and the hypocritical of all denominations; thereby depriving the state of the services of many valuable members, but affording no security against any one unprincipled individual.

IV. That

APPENDIX.

VI. That it is a duty incumbent not only on all Protestant Dissenters, but on those of the established church, and all others who concur in the principles we have stated, to exert their united efforts, by all lawful and peaceful means, to procure a repeal of those laws, which tend to subject numerous and deserving bodies of men to unmerited disadvantages, to deprive the state of the services of many of its most faithful and conscientious subjects, to pervert a sacred christian rite from its proper objects, to violate the principles of the best and freest constitution in the world, and to dishonour one of the first Protestant churches of Europe with an imputation of intolerance and persecution, peculiarly injurious to the interest and honour of the Protestant religion, at a moment when our catholic neighbours are holding out an example of the most free and liberal toleration.

VII. That we have received, with heart-felt satisfaction, the testimonies of approbation with which our conduct, in the former applications to parliament for the relief of the Test Laws, has been honoured; and perceive, with the utmost pleasure, that spirit of zeal and unanimity which pervades the whole body of Dissenters throughout the kingdom, which is still heightened by assurances of approbation and concurrence from many respectable members of the established church. Encouraged by such a prospect, we will adopt and pursue to the utmost of our power every constitutional means to give effect to that spirit, which when firmly and unitedly exerted in the cause of truth, cannot fail of ultimate success in a free and Protestant country.

VIII. That it appears expedient to renew our application to Parliament in the ensuing Session.

IX. That the thanks of this Committee be given to the Chairman, for the ability, zeal, and assiduity, with which, for the space of three years, he has conducted its concerns.

X. That the above Resolutions be signed by the Chairman and inserted in the Public Papers.

EDWARD JEFFRIES, Chairman.

The Committee also came to the following Resolution.

THAT it be recommended to the Protestant Dissenters to shew a particular and marked attention, at the ensuing General Election, to the interest of such Candidates as they *believe* to be well-affected to civil and religious liberty, but especially to such as

being,

being now in Parliament, have *proved* themselves friends to the rights of the Proteſtant Diſſenters *.

* The letter from the chairman, which accompanied the above reſolutions when circulated among the diſſenters, contained the following paragraph, explanatory of this article.

"Permit us to obſerve, that it has been induſtriouſly aſſerted, that we ſeek to impoſe, at the enſuing general election, a teſt in our own favour, upon the candidates for a ſeat in the Houſe of Commons, at the ſame moment that we deſire a religious teſt to be removed from ourſelves. Theſe caſes are by no means parallel; and we conceive, that, in point of fact, the Diſſenters have only reſolved to pay a marked attention at that period to thoſe candidates, who ſhall already have voted in their favour, or who ſhall at that time profeſs their principles and intentions to be friendly to the great cauſe in queſtion. Should the Diſſenters indeed have proceeded farther in ſupport of an unalienable right, ſuch conduct would have been perfectly juſtifiable on the part of the conſtituent towards his repreſentative. But ſince the point at iſſue is ſtill conſidered by many well-meaning perſons as open to a diſcuſſion, which we ourſelves wiſh to promote for the ſake of the general good, it may be adviſeable to expreſs ourſelves ſo clearly on this ſubject, as not be miſunderſtood."

AN ADDRESS

FROM THE

GENERAL COMMITTEE

OF

ROMAN CATHOLICS,

TO THEIR

PROTESTANT FELLOW SUBJECTS,

AND TO THE

PUBLIC IN GENERAL.

www.ingramcontent.com/pod-product-compliance
Lightning Source LLC
Chambersburg PA
CBHW030351170426
43202CB00010B/1334